# A Sense of Self

# A Sense of Self

## Listening to Homeschooled Adolescent Girls

Susannah Sheffer

Boynton/Cook Publishers
HEINEMANN
Portsmouth, NH

Boynton/Cook Publishers, Inc.
A subsidiary of Reed Elsevier Inc.
361 Hanover Street   Portsmouth, NH  03801-3912
*Offices and agents throughout the world*

First issued casebound 1995.
Reissued in paperback 1997.

Editor: Peter R. Stillman
Production: Renée M. Nicholls
Cover design: Barbara Werden
Cover photo by Terry Matilsky

**Library of Congress Cataloging-in-Publication Data**
Sheffer, Susannah, 1964–
    A sense of self : listening to homeschooled adolescent girls /
Susannah Sheffer.
        p.    cm.
    Includes bibliographical references.
    ISBN 0-86709-405-2 (acid-free paper)
    1. Teenage girls—Education—United States.   2. Teenage girls—
United States—Interviews.   3. Teenage girls—United States—
Attitudes.   4. Home schooling—United States.   I. Title.
LC1755.S54   1995
376'.63—dc20                                                    95-18160
                                                                    CIP

Printed in the United States of America on acid-free paper.
99  98  97            EB   1   2   3   4   5

# Contents

# Foreword

*The* girls we meet in *A Sense of Self* offer both hope and challenges for everyone concerned about girls and their often bumpy path to womanhood. Alarming research on girls has been discussed a great deal in the past few years, fueling concern and debate about the pressures and conflicts they face at adolescence. The research rings true with many women, both describing our painful experiences at adolescence and increasing the desire to make things different for our daughters.

Several recent books and numerous magazine articles have created much greater awareness of how girls both silence themselves and are silenced by others, particularly during adolescence. In much shorter supply are suggestions of what can be done, especially by individuals, to combat both the silencing and self-silencing. With this book, Susannah Sheffer opens a new door for those of us who want to make things different for girls.

The possibility of making things different for and with girls excites me. It is the reason my family and I started two new publications, *New Moon: The Magazine for Girls and Their Dreams* and *New Moon Parenting: For Adults Who Care About Girls*. Initially, the magazines were born of my frustration in trying to find some help for both me and my daughters as they approached adolescence. I firmly believed that things should be different. I believed that my daughters should feel *more* powerful as they grew up, rather than less so. They should be able to continue being themselves and not feel forced into abandoning their dreams. Unfortunately, the research did not give me any real guidance about how to make things different. In fact, it made me more fearful.

Susannah's research, on the other hand, presents a different picture of girls at adolescence, a picture that is hopeful.

The homeschooled girls she knows from her work as the editor of *Growing Without Schooling* "didn't sound like people who were losing their self-confidence or distrusting their own voices or burying their hopes and dreams under a facade of compliance" (4). Encouraged by this apparent difference from the prevailing research, she decided to explore whether homeschooling itself was helping girls stay true to themselves in the face of the social and internal pressures of adolescence. The answer is a resounding yes!

Noting that all of the alarming research was conducted on girls who attend school and that some of it zeroed in specifically on the negative influences of school on girls, Susannah chose to look beyond the incorrect assumption that "all girls go to school." She deliberately focused her research "on girls whose homeschooling was characterized by a high degree of choice, autonomy, and control" (8), because she believes that the lack of these factors in school is significant.

But why and how does homeschooling help girls stay true to themselves? And what does that mean for the vast majority of girls who are in and will remain in school? Susannah answers that

> We need to acknowledge the contradiction between what we say we want and what the school system actually communicates. . . . If we want girls to be able to look to their own authority and not always to an external authority, we have to structure school in such a way that it is not always the external authority that holds the answers or determines when something is completed or learned or done well enough. (180)

For girls, looking to their own internal authority is the essence of "speaking their voice." The concept of the true, honest voice explored by Harvard researcher Carol Gilligan and others evokes powerful identification for many women. For me, the work of adults to make things different (and better) for girls consists almost entirely of listening to girls and their voices and then taking the action we can as adults to make change. This can be an uncomfortable thing to do, accustomed as we are to dismissing girls' feelings, concerns, dreams, and opinions as childish. However, it can also be a marvelous thing with wonderful results, as the girls in this book tell us.

Putting the fate of *New Moon* in the hands of girls ages eight to fourteen has also shown me the effect such trust has on girls. At first, the Girls Editorial Board held back, expecting the adults involved to tell them what to do and how to do it. However, as we got to know and trust each other, they were willing to express more and more of their opinions, even when they disagreed with us and each other. I believe it is the total investment of the girls' true selves in the magazine that has made it work.

Harvard researcher Annie Rogers says, "Really listening to girls threatens the fabric of society." That is the challenge *A Sense of Self* presents to the reader. If you're reading this, you care deeply about girls and what happens to many of them at adolescence. You may be looking for ways you can help one specific girl or several girls. You'll find both hope and inspiration in these pages. Making change isn't easy, but it is possible day by day as we listen to girls, respect their self-knowledge and personal strengths, and help them bring that knowledge and strength intact into the world.

Being true to yourself is often difficult, as adults can attest. The only thing more difficult, especially in the long run, is being untrue to yourself. This is something the girls in *A Sense of Self* describe with great self-awareness. Perhaps my favorite part of the book is chapter 7 where Gabrielle, describing how she's changed as she gets older, says, "I'm trying to set my priorities, and now there's a new factor in it, the female part, and how important that is, what it means" (143). Wonderfully, to Gabrielle *being female means being herself*, not being the exaggeratedly confining caricature of femaleness in which teenage girls are encouraged to submerge themselves.

Gabrielle and the other girls whose voices we hear so strongly give me hope for my daughters and other girls. They inspire me with their individuality, self-knowledge, and self-trust, qualities I would still like to have more of myself. Susannah Sheffer has opened a new door for those of us who want to make things different for girls, and I thank her from the bottom of my heart. Now each of us must decide how to go through that open door in our own lives.

Nancy Gruver

# Acknowledgments

This book would not exist if fifty-five girls had not been willing to share some of their most personal thoughts and feelings with me, and I am more grateful than I can express for their time, their trust, and their insight. My promise to respect the girls' privacy meant that when I emerged from each interview session I could not exclaim publicly about the details of what had been said or how fascinating I found it. This book is that exclamation. I am also very grateful to the parents who arranged some of the sessions and in several cases offered their own homes as welcoming places in which to conduct them. I am equally grateful to Holt Associates/Growing Without Schooling. My work there provides the context, the stimulation, and the flexibility that allow me to take on projects such as this one.

I owe great thanks to the people who answered my many questions and addressed my many concerns when this book was only an idea: Carol Sperry, whose vote of confidence was continually reassuring; Lise Motherwell, whose advice about interviewing I deeply appreciated; and Annie G. Rogers, who gave me her time and allowed me access to the interview protocol that she and her colleagues at the Harvard Project had used, a generosity that made it possible for me to turn an idea into an actual book.

In addition, I wish to thank Peter Stillman, one of those rare editors who cares deeply about writing and knows how to help a writer get busy producing some. He too believed in this book when it was only the germ of an idea, and I am grateful for his faith and confidence. I am also grateful that Heinemann Educational Books is staffed with people who make working with a publishing house a delight rather than a struggle.

"No passion in the world is equal to the passion to alter someone else's draft," said H. G. Wells. I am lucky to have such passionate friends, and this book is far better because of that passion than it would have been otherwise. I am also thankful for the time these friends spent talking with me about the issues in this book. This book grew out of delicious conversations with Natalie Rusk over Asian food, with Nancy Wallace over coffee and bagels, with Nancy Gruver (and later Joe Kelly too) over iced cappucino, and with Grace Llewellyn over home fries. Each of these people took (and still take) time from their own important work to eat and talk with me, giving me the kind of exchange and support no institution could rival.

Finally, both this book and my life have been deeply enriched by the perspective and insight of my husband, Aaron Falbel. To paraphrase E. B. White, it is not often that someone comes along who is a true soul mate and an astute critic. Aaron is both.

# Introduction and Methodology

*I* am standing on the railroad platform waiting for Jane to arrive. I have known her since she was a little girl; now she is sixteen, and I haven't seen her in about two years, though we have written and spoken often. She is coming for a visit, and on the phone her mother has warned me, "You won't recognize her, Susannah. She's so grown-up!"

When the train pulls in and the passengers spill onto the platform, I see Jane immediately, walking toward me on long legs with her hair tied back and her bag slung over her shoulder. Yes, she has grown up, and yes, I still recognize her. There is the sense of woman about her, but also very much the sense of girl. Why do I look at her and *not* think loss, not think awkwardness, not think of what a difficult time adolescence is? Stubbornly, perhaps, or maybe because I am truly responding to what I see, I look at her and feel only celebration.

In another city, I am having lunch with Meredith, a girl I have corresponded with for months but have only just met. I know that Meredith holds opinions—has ways of seeing things—that are different from many people, including many of her friends. I think about how difficult that is, how lonely it can feel. "Isn't it hard," I ask her, "to listen to friends be so caught up in something that you don't think is important at all?" "No," Meredith says, surprising me. "That doesn't have to be hard. If it really matters, I listen because it's important to *them.*"

In a weekly discussion group of adolescent girls, I am the adult facilitator listening as the girls talk about how they've changed over the past two or three years. "I feel so much better about myself now," one says. The others agree. "Now I know

*1*

who I am, what I'm good at, what I want to be doing," they say. They talk about becoming stronger, more sure of themselves, less worried about what other people think.

Fourteen-year-old Nicola, a violinist, is in a class with several other girls. They all play a piece, and then the teacher asks them to critique their own performance, to say how they have improved and what still needs work. The other girls are uncomfortable about being asked to evaluate themselves; they are unpracticed at it and they seem unable to avoid turning to the teacher and saying "Right?" or "Do you think so?" Nicola is the only one who seems to find the assignment natural.

When I think about the adolescent girls I know, I see Jane's confidence and exuberance, Meredith's willingness to maintain friendships despite differences, Nicola's ability to look to her own authority for answers, and the girls in the group talking about gaining ground rather than losing it. Nowadays, it is unusual to look at adolescent girls and see these qualities. Recent studies and reports have suggested that adolescence is hard on girls in some particular ways, and news of this research seems to be everywhere. Carol Gilligan and her colleagues in the Harvard Project on Women's Psychology and Girls' Development have written about adolescent girls' "loss of voice" and increasing distrust of their own perceptions. At about age twelve or thirteen, these researchers say, girls begin to doubt themselves and what they know.[1] The American Association of University Women (AAUW) put this idea in terms of self-esteem: in their research, girls were less likely than boys—and less likely as they grew older—to agree with the statement "I'm happy the way I am."[2] Furthermore, the AAUW report "How Schools Shortchange Girls" and the subsequent book *Failing at Fairness* charged that schools in particular discriminate against female students and contribute to the difficulties that adolescent girls face.[3]

The awareness of the challenges girls face has become so widespread that there are now several serious efforts to help girls resist or counter these difficulties.* Among these efforts is *The Mother Daughter Revolution*, a book by Elizabeth Debold, Marie Wilson, and Idelisse Malave. The authors sum up its findings as follows:

> Girls' self-esteem plummets at adolescence, marking the profound intersection of the personal and political in women's development. While younger girls are strong, outspoken, and clear about themselves, at the edge of adolescence they begin taking in what they are told about how girls *should* be and come to see how women are treated in this society. At first, they resist, continuing to trust themselves. They question the accommodations to goodness and niceness increasingly demanded of them. But they become overwhelmed by how little they feel valued and trusted by adults, by the idealization and exploitation of their budding sexuality, by violence, and by increasing injunctions to be silent. Too often, they give up their resistance and give in to what society wants them to be.[4]
>
> ... [A]dolescent girls, as a group, are suffering deeply. Just as the world opens to them, many girls find themselves psychologically distressed. Recent large-scale studies of adolescent health indicate that adolescent girls suffer more from depression, disturbances about their appearance, eating disorders (from anorexia to obesity), and other manifestations of psychological stress than adolescent boys do.... Researchers have described what is happening to girls as "a picture of quiet disturbance" because adolescent girls and boys differ in their ways of experiencing distress. Boys tend to act out, to throw their distress onto the world around them through delinquency and aggressive

* For example, Take Our Daughters to Work day, created by the Ms. Foundation, in which women are encouraged to take girls into their workplaces to give them a greater sense of what women do and can do; Operation Smart, a program sponsored by Girls, Incorporated, which is designed to increase girls' comfort with science, math, and technology; Riot Grrrls, an activist network of girls whose credo, according to a *Newsweek* article, is "We are mad at a society that tells us that girl = dumb, girl = bad, girl = weak"; and *New Moon: The Magazine for Girls and Their Dreams*, which is discussed in chapter 2. In addition to being commendable and interesting in their own right, these efforts also show the extent to which the research on girls has permeated the culture.

*3*

acting out. Girls, however, tend to take their distress into themselves, to internalize it and become anxious or depressed.[5]

In other words, adolescence is hard on both boys and girls, but it is hard on girls in some particularly insidious ways. Because a girl who is suffering inside may seem well adjusted (i.e., nice and quiet) on the outside, it is easy to miss the disturbance she is in fact experiencing.

As the findings of all of this research became known, I was intrigued. I wondered why the girls I knew best and worked with most closely didn't seem to conform to the researchers' descriptions. These girls are homeschoolers—that is, they learn at home and in the surrounding community rather than in schools. As editor of the magazine *Growing Without Schooling* (GWS), I often received writing from homeschoolers, among them many adolescent girls. They wrote about their interests and activities and sometimes about their educational philosophy and outlook on life. In doing so, they inadvertently contributed to the more general discussion of adolescent girls' mental health and self-esteem that was going on among psychologists, teachers, parents, and others who worked with girls. In their letters and essays, the girls who wrote to GWS made comments like these: "I can do anything I put my mind to"; "I am at peace with myself"; "I enjoy standing out; I don't like the idea of being just like everybody else." These writers certainly didn't sound like people who were losing their self-confidence or distrusting their own voices or burying their hopes and dreams under a facade of compliance as so much research was suggesting girls at just these ages were inclined to do. On the contrary, the girls I was hearing from seemed to be expressing a strong sense of who they were, what they believed in, and what they felt capable of. I wondered whether the experience of homeschooling might be giving these girls tools for resisting traditional expectations and challenging various norms.

What people say when they write to a magazine may not

represent their entire state of mind, of course. Yet my sense that these homeschooled adolescent girls were not conforming to the descriptions of the adolescent girl population as a whole was further strengthened by my own direct contact with several such girls. I worked for several years as a writing mentor to homeschoolers around the country, and most of these students were girls. They would send me their stories, poems, or essays and ask for my critical response. Several of them also asked me questions about my own writing or about writing in general.[6] In this work I was struck repeatedly by the self-confidence and the self-knowledge of these girls. Over and over again they taught me about how people find their own voice as writers and how they develop a sense of their own best working processes. Over and over again they told me what they thought, even if it contradicted what I had been saying or what I had guessed about their thinking.

I was also the facilitator of a discussion group for teenage homeschoolers in the Boston area, and again most of the group's members were girls. This group was meant to be a supportive place where the homeschoolers could discuss their thoughts and feelings without worrying about how they came across or whether they were portraying homeschooling in a favorable light. Sometimes we discussed homeschooling, sometimes we discussed growing up, and sometimes we discussed a range of other subjects and ideas. Of course, these teenagers had feelings of confusion and frustration. Their lives were by no means perfect nor free of the usual struggles of adolescence. But particularly in terms of the very issues that concerned psychologists and researchers, these homeschooled girls seemed to be coming from a different perspective.

The statements of self-knowledge and self-confidence from longtime homeschooled girls were striking, but perhaps even more intriguing were the comments I began to hear from girls who had spent several years in school and were now homeschooling. In the discussion group, the girls who had left school only two or three years previously spoke emphatically about having changed in that time. A fourteen-year-old girl who had begun homeschooling two years before said, "I feel so much better about myself now than I did two years ago," and a sixteen-year-old who had left school at thirteen talked about how much more liberated she had come to feel in the past three years. As I listened to this discussion, I couldn't help thinking that research done on girls in school was reporting just the opposite—girls were reported to feel less free and less positive about themselves over time.

Meanwhile, girls who wrote to GWS were echoing the sentiments that the girls in the discussion group had expressed. "For the first time in a long time," a thirteen-year-old wrote about leaving school at ten, "I felt free and so much better about who I was."[7] Another thirteen year old wrote, "It was only after I left school that I opened up and made friends,"[8] addressing the criticism, so familiar to home-schooled students, that being out of school deprives them of opportunities to socialize and to form close friendships.

Many homeschooled boys were making similar statements, and some wrote just as eloquently about how school damaged their self-esteem and how being out of school began to revive it.[9] Homeschooling can bring a feeling of intellectual and creative liberation to both boys and girls. Both male and female teenagers can be strengthened by the chance to have greater control over their learning. But the nature of the concerns about girls' development makes the effect of home-schooling on adolescent girls particularly striking. If research suggests that adolescent girls doubt themselves and do not feel identified with their own goals, then it is noteworthy that homeschooled girls express a firm belief in themselves and act accordingly. The liberation, autonomy, and control that homeschoolers of both genders often feel shows up in starker contrast when homeschooled girls are compared with girls in school because it is the latter group that is currently being portrayed as having less of these qualities. I hope further studies will look at how being out of school affects boys, especially boys who were labeled hyperactive or learning disabled in school or whose learning styles in one way or another did not fit the expectations of their teacher.

HAVING HEARD AND read these various comments from homeschooled girls, I wanted to know if homeschooled adolescent girls were really as different as they seemed to be with regard to issues of self-esteem and trust in their own perceptions. If they were, what accounted for the differences? I wanted to find out how homeschooled adolescent girls felt about themselves and about being girls. I wanted to look closely at what it is like for girls to grow up outside of school and, by extension, outside of an experience common to most other young people in the culture.

My goal in interviewing these homeschooled girls was not to discredit the conclusions or interpretations of the problem that the various research studies had put forth, but rather to build on that research by looking at a population of girls that had not before been considered. Some of the research hinted at the possibililty that schooling might be one of the factors negatively influencing a girl's development, and the AAUW research said this outright as it reported on gender bias in the classroom, in standardized tests, and in school programs. Yet even the AAUW research claimed, "All girls go to school."[10] The thousands of girls who do not go to school, among them a growing number of adolescents, had not been taken into account, and yet their experience differs from the experience of girls in school, in some respects quite markedly. As part of the work of understanding girls' development, it seems important to look at girls who are growing up in a whole range of contexts, including those whose daily lives and attitudes toward education are quite apart from the mainstream.

The word *homeschooling* is in many ways a misnomer, however, particularly as applied to the girls in this study. Much of what these girls do occurs outside the home, and very little of it looks like "school," as they themselves will describe in the next chapter. Furthermore, though *homeschooling* is an umbrella term that is used to describe the choice and the activities of thousands of families, in fact these families are very different from one another and *can* be very different because homeschooling is not a monolithic structure with one prevailing set of assumptions.

The homeschoolers who read *Growing Without Schooling* tend to be less inclined than other homeschoolers to follow a preset curriculum, to use school materials, or to give regular assignments or grades. The overwhelming majority of the girls I interviewed were homeschooling in this independent manner. In part this is because that is the group of homeschoolers I knew best and to which I had the most access. But I also chose deliberately to focus on girls whose homeschooling was characterized by a high degree of choice, autonomy, and control because it was exactly these factors that intrigued me from the start. I already believed that the *absence* of these factors in a school setting is significant. I thought that the contrast between homeschoolers and girls in school could best be highlighted and explored by looking at girls whose homeschooling differed from school the most with regard to these factors.

It seems to me that there are actually three ways to look at the experience of any given homeschooler, and I suggest that readers bear these in mind as they consider the responses of the girls I interviewed. First, there is the question of what the girl is missing by not going to school—what experiences she isn't having, what attitudes she is less likely to develop. When I say that the experience of homeschoolers is very different from the experience of students in school, part of what I mean is that homeschoolers are not immersed in that particular "institution" with its assumptions, expectations, and practices. This can be extremely significant. But it is not all there is to consider.

Second, there is the question of what the homeschooler is actually doing and experiencing by being out of school and what kind of help or support she is receiving from others around her. These vary so widely. Two homeschoolers might be similar in that they are both free from some of the discriminatory or restrictive aspects of school but dissimiliar in that one may be getting much more in the way of support from her parents or much greater access to interesting experiences. And even when the experiences outside of school could be characterized as equally healthy and nourishing, they are still likely to be different from one another.

Third, homeschooling in the 1990s is still an act of resistance, of stepping outside the norm, even though this is less true now than it was twenty or even ten years ago. One of the characteristics of being a homeschooler in these times is, inescapably, that one is doing something different, and this in itself may affect homeschoolers' experiences and perceptions. I will explore this question in particular in chapter 3.

THOUGH HOMESCHOOLERS ARE a small minority of the population, and independent, self-educating homeschoolers a still smaller minority, I believe the experiences and thoughts of the girls in this book will ultimately lend a new perspective to our reading of the research about adolescent girls in general. Sometimes it's impossible to see the effect of "schooling" on students because we take so many aspects of schooling for granted and assume that they could never be otherwise. The girls I have interviewed remind us not to take anything for granted because their experiences and their attitudes show us that things *can* be otherwise. Homeschoolers give us a vantage point from which to look at the experience of students in school. It is my hope that after reading about homeschooled adolescent girls, readers will be able to view the earlier research as being not simply about "adolescent girls" but rather about "adolescent girls who go to school." In this way, schooling and its possible effects on girls can be subject to discussion and evaluation rather than being assumed to be immutable.

Debold, Wilson, and Malave write of *The Mother Daughter Revolution* that "a primary theme of the book is resistance. We share with mothers and daughters diverse strategies to resist, that is, to fight against the silencing messages girls receive from the culture."[11] A primary theme of this book, too, is resistance—how girls resist challenges to their sense of self or pressures to be like everyone else and how home-schooling both increases the need for that resistance and strengthens the girls' capacity for it.

I INTERVIEWED TWENTY homeschooled adolescent girls in person. Thirty more answered the same interview questions in writing, and five recorded their answers on audiocassettes that they then sent to me. Most of the girls responded to a notice I had run in *Growing Without Schooling* about my interest in inter-viewing homeschooled girls between the ages of eleven and sixteen who had been out of school for at least two full years. A few of the girls I interviewed had not seen the notice directly but had been approached by the parents of other girls who had already agreed to be interviewed. Most, however, were not only willing to participate but had to make an effort to indicate their interest; rather than just agree when asked, they had to take the time to write in response to my notice. Perhaps this skewed the sample in favor of girls particularly interested in participating. But it seems to me both unethical and unpro-ductive to conduct such personal interviews with girls who are not completely willing and interested, so I did not feel that the alternative was viable.

Some of the girls who ended up doing the interview through the mail had expressed a specific preference for responding in writing. Others used this method simply be-cause I was not able to travel everywhere; I was only able to interview in person girls from states within a reasonable dis-tance from Cambridge, Massachusetts, where I lived. The written responses, however, came from numerous states, with a couple from Canada as well, so in the end the group was geographically diverse.

When I interviewed girls in person, we met in my office or in the home of one of the local families. Usually, one of the girls' families would allow that home to be used for my inter-views with other girls in the area, so while I interviewed a few girls in their own homes, others were in the home of a friend or acquaintance. When I interviewed girls in my area, I used my office or, in one case, my home. Once, when I was interviewing in another city, I used the office of a friend of mine in that area. Although I can't know for sure, these various locations didn't appear to make a noticeable difference in how forthcoming or comfortable the girls were.

I told the girls that several researchers had studied adolescent girls who go to school but no one had yet looked at girls who were homeschooling during these years, and so I had decided to do that. Homeschoolers are used to being asked questions, either in conversation with skeptical relatives and friends or for media stories, so the idea of someone being interested in their experience and perspective did not appear to surprise them. Carol Gilligan writes that when her group began their research in a private school in New York, one of the girls asked, "What could you possibly learn by studying us?"[12] The homeschooled girls gave the impression that they were used to people trying to learn from them or about them. The questions with which they were most familiar tended to be the most basic questions about how homeschooling works, however. I was not asking those typical sorts of questions, and my interviews were confidential, unlike an interview conducted for a newspaper article or radio program. I emphasized that this was not an interview for *Growing Without Schooling* (for it would have been natural for them to associate me with that sort of interview) and that if I wrote about the girls it would be in such a way that their privacy was protected. My sense was that the girls were intrigued with the idea that this was not a typical interview with the familiar set of questions about homeschooling that they had answered many times.

In many respects my work was informed and influenced by the interviews that others have done with girls and women. Annie Rogers of the Harvard Project generously gave me access to one set of questions that the Harvard interviewers had used, and I was able to use that as a guide when constructing my own set of questions. But in many respects my work was different and cannot be directly compared to the work of these other researchers. I worked alone and I interviewed only those girls who responded to my request (with a couple of exceptions, as noted above). I didn't make an explicit effort to find a representative sample of home-schooled girls, although in the end, the group of fifty-five ended up being very diverse geographically and had some racial diversity—though not as much as I would have liked—as well as having a diversity of family composition, parental occupation, and religion. In addition, some girls had been in school before and others had not.

Perhaps the most significant difference between my work and other studies of adolescent girls is that mine was not longitudinal. In most cases I simply conducted one interview. In a few cases I followed up with further questions, especially when I wanted to see how a girl coped with a particular issue over time. But even then, the time span was only a matter of months, not years. I did ask the girls to reflect on how they had changed over the past few years, but a serious longitudinal study of homeschooled adolescent girls remains for someone else to do.

Early on, I struggled with the fact that I knew several of the girls personally, long before I began this project. I think it would be accurate to say that three were close friends of mine and another eight to ten knew me fairly well (and vice versa). The remaining girls were essentially strangers to me, but most if not all were aware of me and of my work at *Growing Without Schooling*. I was not a complete stranger to them, in other words, even when we were meeting for the first time.

When I was interviewing the girls I knew well, I brought a great deal of background knowledge to the interview. Even though I didn't speak of this during the interview itself and asked these girls the same questions I asked the others, I'm sure that the additional knowledge informed my understanding of what these girls said in the formal interview. I'm also fairly sure that their attitude toward me—as a friend rather than as a stranger conducting research—affected how they felt during the interview. In some cases it may have made them more forthcoming than they would have been with a stranger, but in other cases perhaps less so. In the end I decided that since I couldn't pretend not to know many of these girls already—I couldn't act as though I was not already "in relationship" with several of them, to use Brown and Gilligan's phrase—I wouldn't try and, rather, I would hope that this would give me additional insight. I think it has; the better I know these girls, and the more fully I understand the context of the statements they made in the interview, the more authority I have to interpret their interviews and to write about them.

When I felt myself to be looking at essentially the same issues that the Harvard researchers had looked at, I chose to use the same questions that they had used (in the protocol I had been given). Sometimes I made slight changes in wording (for example, the Harvard interview questions sometimes made reference to previous interviews that the girls had given). When I was looking at something slightly different— for example, the specific experience of homeschooling in a girl's life—I constructed new questions.

The questions I worked from read as follows (note that sections III and VI are reproduced directly from the Harvard questions; sections IV, V, and VII are reproduced with some subtitutions and alterations; and sections I, II, and VIII were written for this research in particular).

## Introduction

This interview is different from others I've done with kids because in this case I'm not going to publish your interview with your name on it and won't use it in GWS; rather, I'm asking you these questions so that I can learn from you about how girls think and feel. There are no right and wrong answers to my questions, and everything you tell me will be confidential; I won't tell your parents, the other girls I talk to, or anyone else what you say to me. Later, when I write about this, I may use your words, but I'll use them in a way that protects your privacy.

## I. Basic Information

1. How old are you?
2. How long have you been out of school?
3. How many siblings do you have, how old are they, are they boys or girls?
4. What kinds of work do your parents do?
5. What's it like where you live (small town, country, city, etc.)?

## II. Work and Interests

6. Which of the things you do (activities, projects, whatever) makes you most happy? You can list more than one.
7. Briefly, how did you get involved in the interest/activity?
8. What words describe how you feel when you do it?

## III. Parents

9. How would you describe your relationship with your mother?
10. How are you alike?
11. How are you different?
12. Do you ever disagree about things?
13. What happens when you disagree?
14. Can you tell your mother how you feel and what you really think?
15. What kinds of things are easy to say out loud? what are hard?
16. Are there things you wish you could talk with her about, but can't?

17. Do you talk to someone other than your mother about these things?
18. Is it important to be able to say to someone what you really think?
19. If you could have a wish come true about you and your mother, what would you wish for?

Please answer the same questions about your father (you can call them 9a, 10a, etc.).

## IV. Siblings

20. How would you describe your relationship with your siblings (can be different for different siblings)?
21. How are you affected by your position in the family (oldest, middle, youngest)?
22. How would things be different for you if you were in a different position?
23. If you're an only child, how do you think you're affected by being an only child? How would things be different for you if you had siblings?

## V. Friendship

24. What do you look for in a friend (what kind of friend do you look for)?
25. Do you speak up when you have something to say with a friend or among friends?
26. How important is it to you that your friends agree with you or you with them?
27. How important is it to you that people in general agree with you?
28. Do you ever disagree with your friends but keep it to yourself?
29. Do you disagree with others, but not with your friends?
30. Do you ever defend a point of view that others don't support?

## VI. Choices

Most kids (most people) have been in a situation where they've had to make a hard decision and weren't sure what was the best thing to do. Could you tell me about a time when you weren't sure what was the right thing to do?

31. What was the situation?
32. What made it a hard choice?
33. What kinds of things did you think about when you were deciding what to do?
34. How did you feel at the time?
35. What did you finally decide?
36. Do you think this was the right or best thing?
37. Is there another way to see the problem? would someone else see it differently?
38. Have you learned anything from what you did?
39. What do you think about when you make choices, in general? What do you try to consider?
40. What kinds of choices is it important for you to be able to make?

## VII. Coming of Age

41. What would you call yourself: a young girl, older girl, young woman?
42. When do you think you will call yourself a woman?
43. How do you feel about your body changing or having changed?
44. Do you see yourself differently, or do you think you will?
45. Do you think other people see you differently, or will see you differently?
46. Do you ever talk about being a teenager/growing into women with other girls?
47. If yes, how do they feel?
48. Do you envy boys at all? Is there anything boys can do that you wish you could do?

49. Do you think boys envy you?
50. Do your thoughts and feelings seem different to you now, compared to when you were nine or so? If you're fourteen or over now, do your thoughts and feelings seem different compared to when you were twelve?
51. If you had to describe yourself to someone else, now, what words would you use?
52. What about if you had to describe the way you were when you were nine? When you were twelve (if applicable)?
53. How do you want to be able to describe yourself in ten years? In twenty?
54. Are there any girls close to your age whom you admire?
55. What do you admire about them? What words would you use to describe them?
56. Are there any adult women you admire?
57. What do you admire about them? What words would you use to describe them?

## VIII. Homeschooling

58. Do you have friends or acquaintances who go to school?
59. What do you have in common with them?
60. In what ways do you feel different from them?
61. If you could change one thing about your homeschooling, what would it be?
62. Are there some things you feel people don't understand about you because you homeschool?
63. How would you explain to them?
64. Can you tell about a specific scene that would illustrate what you mean?
65. If you're with friends who criticize you for homeschooling, what do you do?
66. Can you tell about a time when this happened?
67. Are you happy with how you handled it?
68. If someone criticized you today, would you handle it differently?

17

69. Are there times when you feel unsure about your home-schooling, or wish you weren't doing it?
70. If so, what is it, specifically, that makes you feel this way?
71. Have you done, or do you do, anything in response to that feeling?

If you have been homeschooling for only two or three years:

72. Do you feel different now that you're out of school?
73. What words would you use to describe yourself two or three years ago?
74. What words would you use to describe yourself now? (I realize that you may have answered this earlier, but if the question makes you think of anything else, go ahead and add it)

75. Is there anything else I haven't asked that you'd like to tell me?

NATURALLY, WHEN I interviewed girls in person, we often strayed from this set of questions as their answers brought up other feelings and experiences that I then wanted to explore. Also, after doing the first couple of in-person interviews and receiving the first responses in the mail, I realized that a couple of the questions had been poorly worded, so for the remaining interviews I phrased them slightly differently. The question "Do you see yourself differently, or do you think you will?" that followed the question "How do you feel about your body changing, or having changed?" confused some of the girls, who appeared to see it as a separate question rather than as a continuation of the previous question. They would write, "Do I see myself differently compared to what?" not realizing that the question meant, "Do you see yourself differently now that your body has changed, or do you think you will?" This was only confusing to a small number of the girls, but even so I took care to ask it more clearly in the in-person interviews.

In retrospect I also think the question "Do you think boys envy you?" should have been worded "Do you think boys envy girls?" The latter phrasing might have allowed for a more general exploration of whether there is anything about girls or girls' experience that boys might envy. When I tried phrasing the question that way in some of the in-person interviews, it seemed clearer and led to more discussion than it had in the original phrasing.

Though I had a fairly clear idea of the issues that I thought the questions would raise, I asked many of them with the attitude of an interested explorer, not even being sure what territory they would reveal. In asking about whether the girls felt comfortable speaking up and disagreeing with their mothers, fathers, and friends, for example, I was hoping to learn something about how these girls stood with respect to the silencing that Brown and Gilligan describe. Yet I had no expectations about what issues in particular the girls would raise when they spoke about what was easy to say to a parent and what was hard or when they spoke about disagreeing with friends. When I asked about their homeschooling in section VIII, I placed particular emphasis on how they handled questions or criticisms about homeschooling because I knew that most homeschoolers have to field such questions. Yet I didn't know whether my questions would elicit stories of vulnerability and self-doubt or stories of self-assurance and an ability to defend one's position. It seemed to me that the experience of repeatedly being criticized could give rise to either feeling. So while I did indeed have something I was looking for as I asked those questions, I didn't have a specific idea of what I expected to find.

I asked the questions in the "Coming of Age" section to find out how the girls felt about being girls and how they felt themselves to have changed over time, since these are two key areas in which the findings of other researchers have been significant. This is probably the area in which I was least able to predict what I would find. Although I had suspected that these girls would have a strong sense of themselves with regard to their identity as homeschoolers, I had fewer suspicions about how they would feel about being girls or about

*19*

making the transition from girl to woman. This had never been directly investigated or discussed in the material by or about homeschoolers that I had read.

The stories about girls making difficult choices are among the most moving and illuminating in the Harvard studies. It appears that pressures, tensions, and challenges to their sense of self come together most intensely when girls are faced with choices. So many choices seem to be, at heart, about whether to speak up or remain silent, whether to do what you think is right for yourself or what others believe would be right for you. I felt that I could not improve on the set of questions about choices that the Harvard researchers had asked, so I used their questions. I wanted to learn about how these girls coped with pressures, challenges, threats to their sense of self, and indeed the answers to these questions ended up being a significant part of this book.

When I refer to a girl by first name only, that name is a pseudonym. Although some of the girls said they didn't care whether their real names were used, others did. In the interests of consistency and a greater assurance of privacy for the girls and those close to them, I have used pseudonyms for all the girls I interviewed. Throughout I occasionally quote from writing that has been published by a homeschooled girl in *Growing Without Schooling* or elsewhere, and in those cases I use the girl's real name.

# Chapter 1

## *"They cannot understand the freedom"*

*I*n the foreword to the "Shortchanging Girls, Shortchanging America" study, the authors write, "What happens to girls during their school years is an unacknowledged American tragedy. Girls begin first grade with the same levels of skill and ambition as boys, but, all too often, by the time girls finish high school, their doubts have crowded out their dreams."[13] Some of the study's findings were about girls' actual achievements—their standardized test scores, their success in science and math classes. Much of the study, however, is about what girls believe they are capable of— what they feel is true about themselves—hence, the comment about girls' doubts crowding out their dreams. Of course, as the study acknowledged, girls' beliefs about themselves affect what they go on to do and what kinds of choices they make, so the problem is not only one of perception.

It is noteworthy, however, that close studies of adolescent girls in school seem to reveal that even when girls are technically succeeding in school, they experience self-doubt and distrust their own perceptions. Thus, when psychotherapist Lori Stern writes about girls who "begin in adolescence to renounce and devalue their perceptions, beliefs, thoughts, and feelings," she uses as an example a girl who gives "the appearance of well-being" but is in fact struggling inwardly. Stern reports that as Sheila has gone from age fourteen to sixteen she has had to struggle to stay true to herself. In an interview, Sheila talks about not letting people see who she really is, because if she expressed her true feelings, people wouldn't respect her. She explains, "There is always that little part jumping up in the back saying hey, me, hey, me, you are not worthwhile." Lori Stern comments,

> [Sheila] is a successful student at a challenging preparatory school. However, her success is in goals with which she does not identify. She has never dared to examine, much less pursue, her own goals.
> How can psychologists help such girls to pursue their own goals? How can these girls learn to heed their own voices?[14]

These are important questions, and I believe that home-schooled adolescent girls can begin to answer them. The questions are important not just for psychologists but for anyone involved with education because the questions are not (though they might seem to be) just about girls' inner lives. These questions demand consideration of the external structure in which girls live, and this is where homeschoolers can help.

The trouble with saying (as the AAUW study did) that "all girls go to school" is that the statement implies that school itself is a given, a structure so obvious and immutable as to be unworthy of serious consideration. Of course, the studies of teacher behavior and curriculum content look at school's practices, and indeed the research has been critical of these aspects of schooling and clear about urging that changes be made. But the research has not looked at the structure of schooling as a whole.

Homeschooled adolescent girls allow us to look at the structure and assumptions of schooling in an oblique yet potentially very useful way. Homeschooling, both in theory and in the actual experience of it, is often more different from school than most people assume. If we let homeschoolers show us exactly how it is different, some answers to Stern's questions begin to emerge.

People who are unfamiliar with homeschooling usually imagine that it means sitting at a desk at home and having one's parents teach lessons, using mostly school textbooks and workbooks and following a regular schedule. Some homeschoolers do indeed follow this model, at least to some degree, though even they probably spend only a few hours a day on "schoolwork" and the rest on other activities. Other homeschoolers, who don't follow this model at all, know that even their own friends and acquaintances have difficulty picturing what their daily lives are like and how they actually learn. When you ask these homeschoolers, "Are there some things you think people don't understand about you because you homeschool?" they are likely to offer up a ready list of misconceptions that they routinely encounter. Many of these center on the notion that homeschooling must always mean, literally, school-in-the-home:

> Most of the time they either think I have a tutor or that I sit at a desk all day. Then when I tell them I don't sit at a desk, they think I don't learn. *Erika, thirteen*

> People ask me who my teacher is, and get confused when I tell them I mainly teach myself. *Corinna, fifteen*

> Most people don't understand that I never do lessons or use a curriculum or sit down with my parents and do school every day. . . . Sometimes people don't understand that each and every person is a separate mind, a separate being, that what I am is what I have made myself and not what school made me to be, or more importantly, what my parents taught me to be. *Sonya, sixteen*

> They cannot understand the freedom. . . . People are always asking me if doing this or that will interfere with my "school time." I try to tell them that no such thing exists for me, that all the time is "school time" for everyone, not just me. *Carla, thirteen*

> Some people don't understand how I can learn anything without a certified teacher teaching me. *Cynthia, fifteen*

> They don't understand how we can learn enough without taking tests. I mean, they don't really understand that people learn at their own rate . . . it's not the stereotype person that the test companies have put together. *Pia, eleven*

The big thing is, when you mention homeschooling, they think, "school at home," and, like, how many hours a day do you study? . . . They get the mistaken impression that your parents are sitting there teaching you. [They say,] "Oh, I could never do that, I don't get along with my parents." Well, you know, I'm almost never home these days, and it really wouldn't matter if I got along with my parents or not, because you're basically, in our style of homeschooling at least, you're teaching yourself. *Abby, sixteen*

I think it gives, you know, an illusion, to say that I'm home-schooled. I'd rather say that I'm self-taught. *Tessa, thirteen*

Reading the interviews, I sometimes laughed at the variance in the answers to some of the questions. For example, "Are there any adult women you admire?" brought forth the answers Marilyn Quayle, Hillary Clinton, Thelma and Louise, and Anita Hill, as well as mentions of mothers, siblings, and adult friends. These girls lived on farms, in city apartments, and in suburban neighborhoods.* One mother was a family physician and another practiced holistic healing. And yet their daughters kept echoing one another as they explained how homeschooling did not mean having school at home and being taught lessons by one's parents.

With two exceptions, none of the fifty-five girls I interviewed specifically mentioned using a packaged curriculum or correspondence course, though there are many such programs available for homeschoolers who want to purchase them.† Rather than rely on a correspondence school or cur-

---

* Specifically, eleven said they lived in the city, twenty-five said they lived in the country, twelve said they lived in the suburbs, and seven lived in small towns. These designations may often, in fact, overlap; for example, while some of the country locations were obviously extremely rural and very far from any town, others might easily have fit the description "small town" or "suburbs" as well. Similarly, while some of the small towns or suburbs were actually quite rural, others were close to a large city and probably had a more urban feel to them.

† Even the girls who followed a packaged curriculum said that there were things their friends didn't understand about their lives. One said, "A lot of people just, when they find out I'm homeschooled, they naturally assume I'm, like, a lazy bum, you know, sleep until 1:00 every day, talk on the phone, watch TV all day, don't do

riculum manufacturer to assign them tasks and provide them with materials, these girls used library books and resources from the world at large to learn what school calls the basic subjects. Some of the girls used textbooks (though rarely for all subjects); many did not. Some had used textbooks or other traditional school materials at one time and had later stopped; others were only just now beginning to try using such materials. Both such patterns are fairly common among homeschoolers in general. It's common for families to begin homeschooling with a traditional, school-like setup and then gradually become more flexible. It's also common for homeschoolers to pay more attention to what kids in school are doing as they get older and want to concentrate more heavily on academic work or want to prepare for the college admissions process.‡ Common to both patterns is the idea that no matter how one starts out, the method of homeschooling is not fixed. If anything is characteristic of the approach, it's that homeschooling can change as the student's needs and interests change.

The girls' insistence that they teach themselves—that they don't need to follow a curriculum—is the first indication that they see and experience homeschooling very differently from the way most students see and experience school. Because they teach themselves and are not in a classroom setting, homeschoolers probably spend more time alone than many school students do, and this has interesting implications for girls in particular, who may not otherwise be encouraged to enjoy solitude and to value autonomy. Teaching oneself is not synonymous with learning all by oneself, however. Homeschoolers have access to help, to group activities, to all

any work." So it's not just teaching oneself that others have difficulty understanding, but also the notion of being self-motivated, being able to get out of bed in the morning and begin work even without having to attend school.

‡ Another misconception about homeschooling is that homeschoolers will not be able to get into college. As more and more homeschoolers are being admitted to selective universities and colleges (as well as to state universities, community colleges, music conservatories, and art institutes), this charge is being disproved.

kinds of involvement with other people. What is significant is the *kind* of involvement they have. As a fifteen-year-old girl writes in *Growing Without Schooling* magazine,

> I have been studying more on my own in the past few years, and this year in particular. This does not mean that my mother never knows what I study; quite the contrary. She helps expose me to new material, but mostly I let her know when I am interested in something. Then she helps me find information on it. For example, I am really interested in psychology. We have friends who are psychologists and my mother has gathered a lot of information from them. She is also trying to set up a week this summer when I can go help them and observe what they do.[15]

This girl gives us a picture of a particular kind of relationship with an adult helper, one in which the helper gives assistance that has been requested, that furthers the student along her own course rather than defining a path and then prodding the student to follow it. Homeschoolers such as this are on their own in the sense of being independent and self-directed, and they are involved with others in that they draw upon the help and resources of the wider community. When homeschooled girls write about their lives, they often stress the work they do out in the world with others. As they describe this work, they demonstrate that they see it as *their* work, growing out of their interests and goals. Other people are helpful, inspiring, and important, but they are not the ones who tell the girl what to do or how to do it. As two girls wrote in *Growing Without Schooling:*

> I had always been interested in going to an archaeological dig and working. . . . Last year when I was 11 we found out about [a site] which is about ten miles from where we live. . . . When I go to the dig I usually work with Charlotte, the paleontologist, and my mother works in another section. (*twelve-year-old*)[16]

> A friend of our family loved pottery and was very good at it. . . . She invited me to come and work with her. I'd go once a week for about three hours. I'd get there, and she'd be working on the wheel, and then I'd do my own work, and we'd talk while we

worked. I really improved at pottery a lot more than I had while taking lessons at an art center near here, because with twelve children in the class, you can't expect the teacher to help everybody. Also, the teachers there would have one project and that was what you had to do. With [my friend], she'd say, "What would you *like* to do today?" and she'd give me options, and bring in books of different things I could do. (*fifteen-year-old*)[17]

When the girls I interviewed talked about the activities or interests that made them happiest and in which they felt most deeply involved, many of them listed acting, dancing, playing music, playing sports, and doing volunteer and/or paid work. Some also listed more solitary activities such as reading, writing, drawing, and working at the computer, so perhaps the most significant point is that they have time both for solitary, introspective activities and for active, group activities. But because it's easier to imagine homeschoolers working on their own, it's worth taking an extra moment here to emphasize that they have access to many of the group experiences that other kids have—music groups, theater, sports, Scouts, and so on—and have also created groups specifically of other homeschoolers. I have heard of homeschoolers' writing clubs, theater groups, environmental clubs, and teen groups that get together both for socializing and for focused academic activities such as working with lab equipment and visiting historical sites.

There is, however, a sense in which homeschooling is most definitely individualistic, and this has to do with the way it adapts to individual needs and styles. Fourteen-year-old Kate said in her written interview that "homeschooling provides me with so much time to do exactly what I'm most interested in, all the things that I enjoy and want to learn more about."

It should go without saying that having time for one's own pursuits is important for all kids, but there are ways in which it may be especially important for girls. Given that women often believe they must get everything else done for others *before* they try to carve out a little time for themselves, it's heartening to think about girls who are learning about the value of their own interests. Of course, homeschooled girls have household responsibilities, and some complain about not getting enough time with their parents or to themselves because of the demands that younger siblings place on the family. Others may just be busy juggling many different activities and commitments. But many of them nevertheless cite "having more time to do what's important to me" as a crucial benefit of homeschooling.

When I asked the girls I interviewed to tell me which of their interests or activities made them happiest, I also asked them how they felt when they did these things. From their replies, answers to different questions—what makes girls happy during this time of life? what kinds of experiences seem most valuable to them?—begin to emerge.

The most common answer—whether a girl was talking about a physical, group activity like soccer or a solitary, introspective activity like drawing—had to do with becoming totally absorbed in the activity. Debbie talked about being "oblivious to the rest of the world" when playing the piano, and Stacy said, "I am caught up in the melody and the rhythm." Karin said, "If I have a good idea for a drawing, I can be totally caught up in it," and Lynette said, "When I swim I feel like for the two hours that I am there I can forget about everything and not worry about anything and nothing else in the world matters except swimming."

These answers resonate with the experience of anyone who has worked hard at something, but again this kind of experience may have a particular value for adolescent girls. If the culture encourages girls to worry about how they look and seem to others, and if adolescent changes incline girls toward self-consciousness anyway, it's no wonder that the chance to immerse themselves in something other than themselves is especially welcome. Instead of always having to think, "How do I look? What kind of impression am I making?" girls who can be "totally caught up in" an activity have a chance to be free of these preoccupations.

Of course, some of the clichés about adolescence are true. An important task in adolescence is to find out who you are, what you love, where you will find a place in the world. But girls who seem to be most successful at this search are not finding answers to these questions merely by sitting and thinking about them. Rather, they are finding out about themselves through throwing themselves into activities that are not themselves. The two are not in opposition. When talking about what it's like to dance, Alexa said, "You completely lose yourself, but you also find yourself, in the same instant." She also said that dance is "complete freedom" and "completely expressing everything." Gita likes acting because it lets her be any way she wants to be, free of expectations or norms. "When I act I feel really strong, I can yell for my part or I can be small and shy. I can act *any* way I feel like," she says. At a time when so many girls feel constrained and unable to express what they feel, it's no wonder that they welcome the chance to express themselves completely and act any way they feel. When girls feel this kind of connection with an activity, the activity is not really "other than" themselves at all.

Some of the girls said they liked having something that they knew well and knew they were good at. Angela said, "I feel at home" about dancing, and Pia said about writing, "I feel comfortable, scribbling away." Gabrielle said writing makes her happiest because she feels safe doing it. It makes sense to me that during a tumultuous time of life girls would want this kind of safe harbor and the feeling that they were especially skilled with at least one activity. Several of the girls also mentioned liking the feeling of accomplishing something—seven used exactly those words. Susan, who listed "acting" and "figuring out math" as the activities that made her happiest, added, "In math I feel smart, a personal sense of victory."

Many schooled girls, to be sure, have intense interests and passions as well. Girls who go to school may be serious about acting or music. They may have a volunteer job or internship that is important to them.§ The differences, however, are that many homeschoolers have more time to devote to their interests and that they are often able to think of those interests as primary. They are less likely to refer to music as an extracurricular activity or to drawing as an elective, both of which imply a "nonessential" or "peripheral" status. The homeschooler's day, and indeed her life in general, is more likely to be seamless, without the clear distinction between schoolwork and outside interests that other adolescents are encouraged or pressured to make.

THE GIRLS I'VE been discussing value the chance to learn what they want to learn. Homeschooling often gives young people greater control over when and how they learn as well. Within the same family, one child may learn to read at age five and another at age nine. Homeschoolers may be aware of learning the multiplication tables later than children in school are supposed to but learning about the Civil War earlier (or whatever). Thus, they come to question the notion that everyone must learn the same things at the same time, and they also come to recognize that not everyone learns in the same way. As a thirteen-year-old girl told *Growing Without Schooling,*

> My mother likes to learn things by looking at them. She likes to draw things, but I need to hear it rather than see it. When she was teaching me to [mathematically] borrow and carry [years ago], she kept writing it down and I didn't understand it at all. I said, "Just tell me about it," and when she did that, it took me five minutes to get it. That was so helpful.[18]

This girl recognizes that she learns best by listening, and she lets us see how homeschooling can adapt to that style. Perhaps even more important, this girl was able to be an

---

§ I think volunteer work and internships are simply more common among homeschoolers, though, both because homeschoolers have more time to get involved with such activities and because the homeschooling community tends to encourage thinking in these terms. Articles or workshops about homeschooling teenagers often suggest volunteer work or apprenticeships as a way to learn more about particular topics.

active agent in making her homeschooling work. She knew herself well enough to know what was needed, and she felt herself able to speak up and ask for change.

This sense of being an agent, of being in control of one's own education, is also evident in homeschoolers' discussions of how they set their own goals and then work toward them. A fifteen-year-old wrote to *Growing Without Schooling*, saying,

> One of the reasons that [my brother and I] homeschool is that we have the freedom to choose our own goals and then work toward them in our own way. So many of my friends who go to school depend on other people to make decisions for them and then to stay within the restrictions that the other person may set.
>
> A goal of mine is to become an equine (horse) veterinarian some day. . . . To go to vet school you need a background in mathematics and science. I am currently teaching myself algebra. It's very difficult; I often have to go back and reread sections of the book to make sure that I understand what I'm doing. Last year I became confused and got so frustrated with it that I neglected my work, so I have some catching up to do now. I'll keep my goal in mind, though, and keep working towards those higher levels of math.[19]

At age fifteen, Dana spoke for many when she said in her interview, "I'm very in charge of what I'm doing," and went on to describe how she plans her own day, keeping track of the various things she hopes to accomplish over the course of the week or month and pacing herself accordingly. Corinna, also fifteen, recognized that having control over her learning would have implications beyond homeschooling itself. When comparing herself to her friends in school, she wrote,

> I am more concerned about my future, what I'm going to do with my life. I think this is because I have realized that I can decide what I want to do, and do it. Kids in school are told what to say, think, and do from day one, so they have more trouble when they get out in the real world. This is not to say that I think all schooled kids are brainwashed or stupid. I think it's possible to learn something in public school if you try, but it's a lot more fun to be learning without being told how to.

As Corinna suggests, what girls get from homeschooling as an educational practice can then be carried over into their lives as a whole.

I said that the homeschooled girls I interviewed would begin to suggest answers to Lori Stern's questions. These girls, thus far, have described teaching themselves, setting their own curriculum, and developing a strong sense of their interests and passions. They have talked about learning in accordance with their particular style, about being in control of what they do and how they do it. They have talked about setting goals and working toward them. In describing all this, they do indeed come across as less alienated—with greater feelings of power and capability—than someone like Sheila, who as Stern tells us has "never dared to examine, much less pursue, her own goals," and who always hears a nagging voice saying "you are not worthwhile." But if these homeschooled girls do seem more identified with the goals they are pursuing, it is not just because of something in their psychological makeup (although that may be part of it). It is also because their educational system is explicitly about letting learners make choices about what they will learn and pursue. If these homeschooled girls don't seem to be suffering in the ways that girls like Sheila are suffering, it would be foolish to ignore the structural differences between their lives and the lives of girls in "challenging preparatory schools" like Sheila's. We can imagine that a girl feels in control of her life and her education as a result of other psychological factors that may have myriad causes; we can also imagine that she feels in control precisely because her educational method or program or philosophy is characterized by learners being in control—which would make her resulting feelings of control unsurprising. It can be tempting to think of a concept like "feeling in control" or "identifying with one's goals" as primarily or even only psychological, but thinking exclusively in these terms will, I fear, leave psychologists struggling with the problem of how to help girls pursue their own goals without confronting the fact that the system in which the girls are enmeshed mandates precisely the opposite.

THE VERY CONTROL and autonomy that can make homeschoolers feel capable and powerful can also leave them vulnerable to self-doubt, however. Just as homeschoolers are aware of the mainstream perception of homeschooling, so are they aware of how the culture at large looks at success. They cannot avoid learning about the standards by which school students are judged, and they then have to decide how they will stand in relation to those standards. To what extent will they try to measure themselves by school's (and by extension, the culture's) standards or worry if they don't live up to them? To what extent is it possible to step outside the school arena and define success or education in a completely different way?

Some families choose homeschooling precisely because they think it will make it more likely that their children will succeed by conventional standards. They see homeschooling as an unconventional route to a fairly conventional destination, and thus they are happy to cite the high standardized test scores that many homeschoolers achieve or their admission to selective colleges. Yet for others, homeschooling is about not having to measure oneself against others and not having to succeed according to standardized tests or other measurements that seem wholly inapplicable to self-directed, interest-based learning.

When you talk to homeschooled teenagers, you can see that while the parents struggle with these issues in one way, the teenagers struggle in their own way. Some homeschoolers frustrate their rebellious parents by worrying more about how they're doing by school's standards than their parents ever meant them to worry. Others frustrate their parents by becoming even more independent and less concerned about these standards than their parents can easily accept. And no matter how ready to disregard school's standards the homeschooler may be, others are still interested in applying those standards. A homeschooler may feel comfortable saying, "I'm not in a grade" or "I don't measure myself by test scores," but she will still have to field questions from friends and relatives who inquire, "How are you doing? Are you keeping up with the kids in school? Where do you stand compared to others your age?"

For most kids and parents, homeschooling seems to be a matter of negotiating the line between what the culture values or expects and the values or expectations that homeschooling itself tends to encourage. Sometimes homeschoolers can't help being drawn into the worries that people seem to expect them to have. Even if they are not themselves vulnerable to those worries, they may still feel the need to explain why they don't think in those terms. When I asked Kendra, thirteen, if she ever felt unsure about homeschooling, she said, "I can't think of a time that I really haven't wanted to do [homeschooling], but there were times that I felt unsure about it, when there were, like, these standards I have to meet." When I asked if she did anything in response to that feeling, Kendra said, "I try to just tell myself, like, that I'm enough, that I don't have to worry about meeting standards that, I mean, I could meet if I have to, but most of them I don't have to." Even if Kendra values precisely the way that homeschooling doesn't measure her against others (as school did), she still has to remind herself that she is "enough," because with external standards everywhere around her, she can't help wondering about their validity now and then.

The same is true for Tina, fifteen, whose closest friends all go to school. Sometimes their influence makes her doubt whether she's learning enough in homeschooling. Her friends will quiz her on algebra problems or ask her if she knows the facts they are memorizing for a test the next day. This quizzing, entirely unbidden, sometimes makes Tina doubt herself and wonder whether she is learning enough. But, she says, "I snap out of that very quickly, because I know that I am." Other people provoke doubts; Tina provides herself with reassurance. She has to look within herself for something to counter her friends' objections.

Yet it's not enough for Tina to make peace with this in her own mind. Because her friends in school *are* constantly being measured and graded according to school standards, they find her freedom from these constraints intriguing and sometimes unsettling. They don't seem able to let Tina be, but instead keep testing her, forcing her to explain again and again that she doesn't like to be tested, that testing isn't how she determines the success of her homeschooling anyway, and that if homeschooling works for her they shouldn't be bothering her with questions designed to check whether she is learning as much as they are.

> I make it clear to them that I don't put up with [testing], and that I don't like to be tested, because, you know, I know what I need to know, and it's none of their business if they don't believe me. . . . I do have friends that [criticize me for homeschooling], and I get very mad at them. They've come out of nowhere and tried to test me on, like, algebra problems, and it's like, "What is this any of your business?"

Even though Tina speaks with confidence and clearly has the strength to handle other people's objections and doubts, she is forced to be self-reflective and sometimes defensive in a way that her friends in school are not. She would like them to be just as self-reflective, and she tells me that she often tries to use her explanations about homeschooling as a way of encouraging her friends to think about the aspects of conventional schooling that they take for granted. Some do. Being friends with a homeschooler can be interesting and thought-provoking in just this way. But because kids in school have major institutions and the beliefs of most people in the culture on the side of their method of education, they don't have to question it and work up arguments in defense of it the way Tina and others like her must do with regard to homeschooling. Again, simply the fact of being asked over and over again "Are you learning enough? Can you really learn that way?" propels homeschoolers into a kind of self-examination that can leave them vulnerable but can also give them a layer of strength and reinforcement that makes them both doubly secure and doubly self-aware.

If kids in school are puzzled by homeschoolers' independence from standard measurements, homeschoolers can be just as puzzled by school kids' preoccupation with them. Sixteen-year-old Madeline remembered growing up with schooled friends who had very different attitudes toward these standards. When I asked Madeline in what ways she felt different from kids in school, she said,

> A couple of my friends thought that if they didn't measure up to the standards at school, then they weren't good enough, and I always thought that that was stupid. So that was probably the biggest difference [between us], that they were always thinking that they had to measure up to some kind of system, and I was always like, "Beat the system—hey, you don't want to be part of that!"

Homeschoolers who have considered these school standards and found them irrelevant or unimportant are freer from external judgments than their peers in school are. Madeline, choosing not to define herself in school's terms, reminds me of a homeschooler who told me she answers the question, "What grade are you in?" with "I'm not in a grade" rather than with "I would be in eighth grade" or "I'm at the equivalent of eighth grade." These homeschoolers are consistently saying, "I don't use that system of measurement." And they are able not just to *say* these things but to live accordingly. A teenager in school might want to say, "I'm not in a grade," but the school would not allow her to act in accordance with that statement. A teenager in school might believe that letter grades or test scores are not accurate measures of her ability, but she would still be immersed in a system that considers those measurements very important. The homeschooler with the same beliefs is immersed in a system (or an approach) with which her beliefs are consistent.

On the other hand, few people are questioning the entire method or feasibility of the educational system in which the schooled teenager is immersed. In that sense, she may feel herself to be on more solid ground than does the homeschooler, who is constantly feeling her education called into question. When a teenager in school succeeds or fails, her own abilities may be on the line, but a homeschooled teenager often feels that an entire educational practice is being judged on the basis of her individual performance. "I know some people are watching to see if I'll fall flat on my face," said a homeschooled friend of mine as she entered college. She was aware that neighbors and acquaintances were at least to some degree watching to see whether the homeschooler would "make it" in the world of college. Although she was able to make light of that burden, it's easy to see how some homeschoolers would feel it more heavily.

Lyn Brown writes, "Doubting what they know, these fifteen- and sixteen-year-old girls look to external authorities to define what is of value and what is legitimate knowledge."[20] This sounds exactly the opposite of the homeschooled girls I've quoted here, who say, "I tell myself that I'm enough," "I know that I am," and "I know what I need to know." Homeschoolers, standing without the solid floor of convention and external authority underneath them, have to construct an internal authority and an individual definition of legitimate knowledge that will be strong enough to support them. As they struggle with these issues and evaluate the differences inherent in the homeschooling approach, many of them end up saying, "Well, there may be those standards out there, but I know what's important to me." They wrestle with doubts and then often end up placing great value on internal authority and on their own definitions of what is legitimate knowledge. So their struggle is important, and what they gain from it they can then carry over into other areas of life and so end up stronger or more trusting of themselves than the adolescent girls Brown describes.

In later chapters, I will explore how this plays itself out in various arenas, but I'll give one quick example now. In the older homeschoolers' discussion group that I lead, girls were discussing familiar concerns about weight and body image. One girl told the group how much she weighed and then said that she often wondered if that was all right. Another girl, a couple of years older than the first, said, "I used to worry about that too, but then I told myself that I'm fine the way I am, and it doesn't matter how other people think I should look." Someone else commented that this sounded much like the conversations they had had before when they had worried if they were doing as much work as kids in school. This girl recalled that in those conversations they had always come back to the idea that they didn't have to be exactly like school kids or to learn exactly what they were learning. Since these girls were already so used to and so good at dealing with pressures to meet an external standard of knowledge, they were then able to see how they could use this ability to deal with the pressure to meet an external standard of beauty. They made the connection between their trust as homeschoolers in internal sources of knowledge and the way that they could extend this same trust as girls to issues such as preoccupations with weight and appearance. This is an important connection to make, and homeschooled girls who can make it are also better off in areas that have nothing to do with homeschooling.

FEMINIST PSYCHOLOGISTS HAVE described the female experience as being out of sync with the assumptions of the dominant (male) culture and not always adequately reflected in descriptions of "human" experience (which is usually male experience). This marginalization of female experience is considered harmful. As Brown and Gilligan write, among the problems that have been seen as "central to the psychology of women" is "the feeling of not being able to convey or even believe in one's own experience."[21] While I would have been ready to agree that the marginalization of one's experience is indeed harmful, homeschoolers challenge my own perception about this. They often seem to me to be able to free themselves from the expectations of the dominant culture, thus needing less validation from it as time goes on. They are able to use their distance from the dominant culture in a way that strengthens rather than weakens them.

A typical homeschooled teenager reads novels and sees movies in which teenagers go to school and school is shown as the central structure in young people's social and even intellectual lives. School is where one comes of age, where one is supposed to discover what kind of person one is. Homeschooled teenagers regularly encounter people who say, "Why aren't you in school today?" or "Do you really think you're learning enough?" and "How will you be able to succeed in life?" This is not what I would call validation of one's experience. Some homeschoolers do doubt themselves because of this, and I'm sure homeschoolers would cheer if a teenage novel or film came out with a homeschooled protagonist. Yet in the interviews I conducted, in the discussion group I lead, in homeschoolers' writings, and in their presentations at conferences and other gatherings, the dominant feeling I perceive is pride in their unusual perspective and gratefulness that they are able to learn in this alternative way. Yes, homeschoolers probably would enjoy seeing their experience and perspective reflected in the culture at large, and some may work toward making this happen by speaking out publicly, but it doesn't always follow that they are suffering without this reflection or validation. Rather than always or only asking themselves how they measure up to school's standards, they are actively calling those standards and assumptions into question.

I am not trying to downplay the negative effects of the various kinds of marginalization that do exist, but I'm trying to look more closely at how the experience of being different from the norm operates under different circumstances. In the AAUW studies of girls' self-esteem, African American girls were more likely to agree with the statement "I'm happy as I am" than were white or Latina girls.[22] Some reports suggest that African American girls are less vulnerable to the stereotype of the nice, obedient, silent girl that is idealized in white and, in perhaps other ways, Latina culture.[23] Furthermore, African American mothers may be more likely to encourage their daughters to resist cultural norms and to help them do so. Debold, Wilson, and Malave write,

Many African American girls manage to hold on to their voices and their belief in themselves in adolescence, more so than white or Latina girls. To do so, they draw on strong family connections and communities, and on the role that women play in those families and communities (although these communities have suffered in the last decade or so as fewer resources have come their way). In a protective but costly maneuver, they distance themselves from schools and other institutions in the culture that tell them they are worthless. This strategy makes for effective resistance in the short term, but in the long run it leaves these girls dangerously outside paths to economic security.[24]

The AAUW study comments on the same issue by saying that "these black girls did not have high self-esteem in areas related to school."[25] In other words, while it appears that African American girls are not suffering through the same kind of "loss of voice" that white and Latina girls are, they are not identifying with the goal of school-based success either.

Most adults consider this a problem, and given our culture's values, it is in some respects. But homeschoolers ask us to consider these questions in another way, particularly those homeschoolers who only left school as teenagers, in a move that is customarily thought of as "dropping out" but which they have chosen to see very differently. The usual dropout who has not derived self-esteem from school and who does not place a high priority on school success may find self-esteem in other arenas but suffer some negative consequences as well— exactly the sorts of negative consequences of marginalization that people usually discuss. A dropout may be deeply affected by the knowledge that she is unable to succeed in the traditional academic or social arena of school or that the ways in which she does succeed are not valued by the culture.

Girls who become homeschoolers as teenagers often tell a story of learning to listen to their own voices, of not forcing themselves to become what others believe they should be, and of getting their parents to support their resistance to these pressures and to help make a different kind of life possible.

Many dropouts may feel all of these things also, but homeschoolers more often have a framework and a support system that confirms their perceptions and allows them to see the act of leaving school in a positive way. Homeschoolers are able to replace school with (to varying degrees) a community that welcomes them and applauds their adherence to their own intuitions and their courage to try something new. Perhaps most important, this community has already developed a sophisticated critique of schooling, so it encourages teenagers who leave school to fault the school system rather than themselves. This is often a radical shift for a teenager who has previously thought, "There's something wrong with me for not being able to succeed in school." It's also a radical shift for parents who have become accustomed to thinking in terms of their child's deficiencies rather than the system's.

In addition to the support and shift in attitude that the homeschooling community offers teenagers who leave school, writers and thinkers within that community (as well as in the school reform movement in general) have questioned the connection between schooling and job qualifications. They would not be so quick to agree with the statement that resisting school leaves one dangerously unemployable (or less employable). This critical look at some of the assumptions about schooling might help dropouts view their decision in a different way, as it has helped homeschoolers. There is an overlap here, a way in which homeschoolers and the homeschooling community can be useful to dropouts.

Jane O'Reilly considers the question of girls' loss of self-esteem in an article for a popular magazine, and she quotes Janie Ward, a member of the Harvard project, who says that

> when an African-American girl switches on the television set and sees that "perfection" is thin, blond, and tall, the difference is so great that she is forced to self-create, to say, "That's not me" and to affirm herself as a member of her community. "In healthy black families," says Ward, "children are helped to develop the ability

to repudiate outside notions." Black mothers can be strong, competent role models who socialize their children to know that racism is not the result of something wrong with black people but the result of white people's problem with black people.

Resistance to the dominant culture may be great for personal self-esteem, but it is not something school administrators understand as a valuable indication of future promise. Black girls, confronted with a demand for conformity that they recognize correctly as irrelevant, disrespectful, and boring, may simply choose to drop out. They see no connection between school and their own future. Unhappily, they choose the kind of resistance that is oriented toward short-term survival instead of long-term liberation.[26]

Like the others I've just quoted, O'Reilly recognizes the strengths that can come from being able to resist the expectations of the dominant culture and from receiving familial support for doing so. She sees that school doesn't welcome this kind of resistance and therefore concludes that the "self-creating" that African American girls are forced to do is beneficial in the short run but eventually harmful.

If a girl sees no connection between school and her own future or sense of herself, that is a problem only if she assumes that going to school is the only legitimate way to spend one's adolescence and the only route to a healthy and productive adult life. Once that assumption is questioned, the girl's resistance takes on a different cast. Resistance to school and school's norms need not be only a short-term survival tool.[27]

WHEN IT COMES to issues of choice, agency, identification with one's goals, learning in accordance with one's individual style, and determining whether or not to measure oneself by external standards, we can look at the experience of students in school and then explore, as I have tried to do, how the experience of homeschoolers differs. But the reports about girls in school have dealt with other issues as well. The AAUW research and the book *Failing at Fairness: How Schools Cheat Girls* look at the discrimination girls face within the school context. Yet precisely because the discrimination is dependent upon a school context, there is often no parallel situation to examine within the homeschool setting.

Observers have noticed that teachers call on boys much more often than on girls, for example, and give boys more attention in other ways. Homeschoolers don't get "called on" at all. Homeschooling simply doesn't operate that way. The less closely the home school operates according to school's assumptions and methods, the harder it is to make direct comparisons. For the girls I quoted earlier, who see themselves as self-educators and their parents as helpers and resources, there is no instruction as there is in the classroom. It is not only the "called on" student who gets to participate or learn. Instead of being called on or made in other ways subject to the decisions of the teacher, these self-educating homeschoolers are learning through reading, through pursuing activities outside their homes, through seeking out information, and through interaction with other people.

There is no parallel situation to examine, and that is precisely the point. That is the reason that these homeschoolers do not and cannot possibly suffer the kind of gender discrimination that this example describes. Similarly, Carol Gilligan has written about women's opportunities to ally with girls as they resist pressures to silence themselves, even when resisting these pressures might cause conflict. In some of Gilligan's key examples, however, there would not even have been a need for resistance in the first place if the girl had not been a student in school. One story is about Anjli, who offered an unusual interpretation of Marvell's poem "To His Coy Mistress." When Anjli's paper was graded by other teachers in a cross-grading exercise, they gave it a poor grade, saying that Anjli didn't understand the poem. Her teacher defended Anjli's interpretation—in effect, her perspective—even at the risk of conflict with her colleagues.[28] I admire both Anjli and her teacher, but I can't help thinking that without assignments and grades, the entire challenge and the consequent need for resistance would never have arisen.

The structure of the educational system in which Anjli and her teacher found themselves is what gave rise to the situation that then made their resistance necessary. The self-educating homeschooler, in contrast, can read Marvell's poem and come up with any interpretation she pleases. If she discusses the poem with a friend or her mother or an adult mentor or other homeschoolers in a discussion group, or if she reads the literary criticism that has been written about it, she might discover that her interpretation is different from others'. But nothing would tell her that she was *wrong*. Not only would she be likely to think, in a general sense, that different opinions were acceptable (see chapter 3), but there would also be no structural mechanism (i.e., a poor grade) for telling her that her interpretation was faulty.

This is not to say that homeschoolers have no opportunities or need for resistance—on the contrary, they have many such opportunities, and throughout this book I explore them. But I think it's important to understand that some kinds of pressures and some kinds of occasions on which girls might "lose voice" are entirely school based.

Other kinds of occasions and opportunities for discrimination are not as exclusively school based, though they are often dependent on the school context to a large degree. The question of whether the curriculum or the syllabus is biased is a case in point. Most of the girls I interviewed did not follow a curriculum, either purchased or parent designed. They did not receive reading assignments, so the question of whether there are more male than female authors represented in their assignments (as well as other potential instances of bias) does not arise.# But it is certainly true that parental inclinations and biases influence what books and materials are available and perhaps even which ones are recommended to the young people. This is probably of greater importance when home-schoolers are younger, since by the time they reach the age of

# For those who do use a packaged curriculum, this would at least potentially be an issue.

the girls in this study, they are commonly choosing their own reading material and have contact with many people outside the family who can recommend and discuss books. Nevertheless, the effect of the parents' tastes, opinions, choices, and biases can't be dismissed.

The question, however—and to me this is a question that remains open—is whether a school curriculum or a parental assignment (or even parental suggestion) carries more weight in a student's mind. On the one hand, I'm inclined to think that a state-mandated or even teacher-chosen curriculum carries with it a greater aura of authority, so that a student would be more inclined to think that books assigned as part of such a curriculum were the important books, the ones that counted. In that case, omissions from that list of books would also be significant, as critics charge when they argue that not enough female writers or writers of color are represented. Furthermore, many students read only what their school assigns them, whether because they have a limited amount of time in which to read or because they become turned off and disinclined to read when it is not required. When students read only what school requires, omissions from a school curriculum become even more significant. In keeping with this view, I tend to think that a parental suggestion or even a parental assignment carries less of that aura of objective authority. I tend also to think that homeschoolers, especially those not following a curriculum, make fewer (or no) distinctions between being in and out of school or between schoolwork and other work. Thus, they are probably less likely to think that what is in a curriculum or what is assigned or suggested by their parents is the sum total of what ought to be known or can be known.

On the other hand, perhaps the opposite is true. Perhaps parental opinion strikes some young people as more persuasive and authoritative than the school curriculum. In that case, perhaps homeschooling parents have an even greater responsibility than do school teachers or administrators to make sure that the books and materials they choose or have available are not discriminatory. Also, when homeschoolers don't have or have less access to outside influences and resources, parental inclinations and choices take on greater significance. Furthermore, when homeschoolers don't see themselves as self-educators, as able to seek out their own information (as the girls in this study seem almost unanimously to see themselves), parental choices again bear greater weight.

Thus, the question of whether discrimination through curriculum content affects homeschoolers still seems open to me and dependent upon a great many variables. The same is true of the question of whether homeschooling parents convey gender bias in other ways—perhaps giving more encouragement to boys, for example, or holding a different set of expectations about sons and daughters. This could certainly be true in homeschooling families (as in any family). The girls I interviewed did not express resentment about brothers' getting more attention or parents' having goals for their sons that they did not have for daughters. In a couple of cases, the girls mentioned when speaking about siblings that their parents treated all the kids in the family equally. But as the research about bias and discrimination in school shows, it is not enough to ask people whether these things occur. *Failing at Fairness* is full of stories about teachers who swore they treated boys and girls equally and were then shocked to see a videotape of their own behavior. Some kinds of bias can only be observed (or can be observed more easily) by an outsider, and perhaps someone will undertake to observe homeschooling families with this in mind.**

---

** Anyone doing this would have to take into consideration the fact that the situations under observation would not be parallel, as I've been saying here. In many home schools there are no lessons, no "teacher behavior," in the way that there is in the classroom. One would be looking at family behavior and interaction for the most part.

# Chapter 2

## Family Context

*F*amilies who choose homeschooling are opting for a traditional family setup in which the father works outside the home and the mother doesn't. For this reason, homeschooling is often regressive and not suited to less-traditional families. Also for this reason, homeschooling is likely to foster traditional sex roles in children and teenagers.

Do you believe this? Many people do. Many people would assume that I wrote that paragraph in all seriousness, without a trace of irony, and that the ensuing discussion would be about how homeschooled adolescent girls are affected by growing up in families with traditional gender roles and traditional American work arrangements. I would have to discuss the fact that homeschooling is only possible for a limited number of families, since it is clearly unworkable for single-parent families and families in which both parents work outside the home.

I interviewed fifty-five girls from forty-nine families, and of these thirteen described their mothers as having paid jobs (many of these part-time), a few others mentioned that their mothers do volunteer work either outside the home (such as "volunteer tour guide at museum") or from home ("runs local homeschool association"), and the rest responded with some variation of "stays home with us," "homeschools us," or "doesn't work outside the home." Five of the mothers were single parents. In a couple of the single-parent families, the girls saw their fathers regularly; a couple of others saw their fathers only occasionally, and one had not seen her father since she was very young.*

Does this information mean that homeschooling families fit the stereotype of the two-parent family with the father working outside the home and the mother not working for pay? On the one hand, the numbers do suggest that this situation is common. On the other hand, they suggest that it is not universal. They disprove the claim that homeschooling is impossible for single-parent families or that homeschooling mothers cannot also work outside the home.

*Growing Without Schooling* has published several stories from single parents about how they manage to work at home, work outside the home at jobs to which they can sometimes bring their children, or arrange for their children to spend time with relatives, friends, other homeschoolers, and in group activities run by adults other than the parent.[29] Similarly, two-parent families have written about how they have arranged their work schedules so that one parent is always available, have arranged for their children to spend time with other adults, or are able to bring their children with them to work some of the time.[30] Furthermore, both mothers and fathers have written about running home businesses or otherwise working at home.

The age of the children influences the family's arrangements to a large degree. Several of the adolescent girls I interviewed had younger siblings, so that while they themselves

---

* The fathers' occupations were as follows: real estate salesman, microbiologist, teacher (three), chemist or chemistry professor (two), railroad worker (two), computer executive, millwright, artist, newspaper publisher, musician (two), administrator, craftsman, lawyer (two), computer consultant (two), public official, housepainter, pilot (two), firefighter, carpenter, furniture salesperson, government worker (two), remodeler (homes), sales manager, cook, writer, "does odd jobs," engineer (three), construction worker (two), postal worker, graphic designer, electrician, house manager of theater, jeweler, welder, code enforcement officer, and educational consultant. The occupations of the mothers who were described as having paid jobs were as follows: works at grocery store, works at bookstore, physician, hairdresser, word processor, college English teacher, communications consultant, librarian, runs family daycare, physical therapist, writer/publicist, holistic healer, and jeweler.

were involved in outside activities and didn't require constant parental attention when they were at home, the family's work arrangements had to accommodate the younger children as well. When the family did not have younger children, the mother was more likely to be working outside the home some or much of the time.

But although the matter of logistical arrangements is important, it is not all there is to consider. To me, there are deeper questions that are less often examined: How do homeschooling families see themselves, whatever their work or financial arrangements might be? Do the families who seem to be arranged according to traditional gender roles actually view themselves as traditional? Do the children in these families absorb traditional attitudes toward work and toward gender roles? What else is at issue or comes into play when homeschooling is part of the picture?

Even before I considered the responses of the girls I interviewed, I had information that helped me think through these questions because homeschooling parents have been discussing these topics for some time. It is clear to me that there are not one but several answers to each question.

When a woman fits the description of "a housewife" or "a wife and mother," without any other work attached to the phrase, what is the effect of adding homeschooling to the equation? If the woman doesn't feel that she has actually made the choice to teach her own children but has felt pressured to do it by her husband or her church community, she may see homeschooling as yet another burden—the dishes, the laundry, and the teaching of the kids as well. On the other hand, many women in this sort of family see homeschooling as making their lives as "housewives" or "stay-at-home mothers" more meaningful. As a pioneering homeschooling mother said on a popular television talk show in the early 1980s, "I don't want to just cook for my kids and clean up after them and let someone else do all the interesting stuff"—namely, being involved with their growth and learning. Homeschooling can allow a mother to use her intellect and creativity in ways that she hadn't when she viewed herself only as a caretaker or custodian, and many women report this perspective.

It is also possible—even in combination with this positive feeling—for a mother to feel she is homeschooling at some personal sacrifice. She may homeschool because she believes it is good for her children, and indeed it may truly be good for them. But no matter how pure the mother's motives, she may feel some resentment that her children are freer or more able to pursue their own interests than she is. The freer the homeschooling is and the more the children are able to be self-directed, the more the mother may have to confront the question of her own interests and work. Often homeschooling families start out by trying to replicate school in the home, with the mother planning lessons and giving assignments. But as the structure evolves into something that looks much less like school, the mother has to reinterpret and reinvent her role. Think of the girls in the previous chapter who described teaching themselves and not needing their parents' constant input. The mothers of these girls cannot see their job solely as "homeschooling parent" because such a job no longer requires their full-time involvement (or never did). As the children become more independent and self-directed, the mothers (or in some cases both parents) are often prodded into a deeper investigation of their own role. Even if they hadn't thought in these terms before, it is now necessary for them to have something of their own to do and something else with which to identify. There is no doubt that this process can be painful on both sides. Debold, Wilson, and Malave write about how destructive a mother's resentment of her daughter's opportunities can be—and how difficult it is for mothers to negotiate this balance.

> Not only do the daughter's opportunities raise questions about the necessity of a mother's choices, but the daughter's very different strategies can cause anxiety in the mother for the daughter. A mother's feelings about her daughter's life choices may, thus, become a very complicated mixture of anger, anxiety, and

jealousy. . . . [T]hese feelings will often confuse a daughter: Can she explore the world freely with her mother's blessing? Or will her success in the world be at the cost of her mother's love? Daughters are placed in a double bind of potential betrayal of themselves or their mothers when these thoughts and feelings are not acknowledged and brought into conversation. Daughters often want to tell their mothers, "Explore your own desires—'Get a life.'"[31]

Indeed, some of the girls I interviewed were aware that they were freer or felt better about themselves than their mothers did. In answer to the question, "How are you and your mother different?" Meredith, sixteen, wrote, "My mother has a lot less self-esteem than I do. I sometimes think she is amazed by how confident in myself I am." Susan, fifteen, wrote, "I think I'm a little more centered with what I want in life than she is." Furthermore, homeschooled daughters may turn out to be not only more self-confident than their mothers but also more different from the norm—or simply from their mothers—in ways the mothers had not anticipated. Homeschooling mothers may intend to raise daughters who are different from themselves in at least some ways, but they may be surprised by how different they actually become. The daughters don't just reflect their parents' beliefs, but rather absorb from them and from the process of homeschooling an attitude of critical questioning and a refusal to take various norms for granted.

Sixteen-year-old Sonya, for example, has two loves, bluegrass music and basketball, and in both cases she is often the only female player. She is aware that her comfort in these arenas often surprises her mother.

> I am the only girl on a [basketball] team of eight boys, and last Saturday I played a team of all boys, which made me the only girl on the court during two halves of the game. To tell you the truth, I don't mind in the least that I am the only girl. I know many girls who would rather die than do what I am doing, many girls who wouldn't even play on a team of all girls unless they knew at least one other player. . . . One thing that sets me apart

from most girls is the fact that growing up, some of my best friends have been boys, and even today I find that it is easier for me to get along with boys vs. most girls my age. Since there really aren't many girls who like basketball (who are seriously into playing it) I've always played informally with boys anyway, so it's nothing new for me.

Mom doesn't understand why I keep playing. She turned white in the face when I told her I was the only girl on the team, and she thought that I would quit. She *wanted* me to quit. She's told me some about what she was like when she was my age, and she sometimes expects me to be just like she was, or more like girls today, and I'm neither. She's often told me that when she was my age, she would have been too scared or shy to do the things I do today. I've got the competitive instinct that Mom says only boys are supposed to have.

. . . When I find that I'm not one of the best players, that I'm not physically strong enough to fight for the rebound under the boards, don't have hands big enough to handle the ball really well, it just makes me want to get better. I'm constantly trying to eliminate my weaknesses, and the end result is that I'm a competitive perfectionist . . .

The boys on the team are somewhat shy and unsure of me, but once they get to know me better I'm sure things will go well. I've been in situations like this before and in the end, things have always turned out for the best. Mom confessed another of her fears to me: she said she was worried that the other players would end up being mad at me if I wasn't as good as they were. First of all, I told her that would never happen, but if it did, I'd get mad at them, and when I get mad I get better at basketball. So things, again, would turn out all right in the end.

It's undoubtedly challenging for a mother to accept that her daughter is quite different from her or has made different choices. Debold, Wilson, and Malave write, "[A] daughter's difference can feel like a pointed statement about a mother's choices."[32] What complicates these issues for some home-schooling mothers is that, as I said, they truly did intend their daughters to be different and to question assumptions. But because this questioning is so very much a characteristic of at least some types of homeschooling, and because it is the daughters who are being raised as homeschoolers and not the mothers, it is inevitable that some daughters end up prodding their mothers to question even further than the mothers had intended. Girls who are comfortable with being different may be comfortable challenging sex-role stereotypes even though that wasn't at all what their mothers planned on when they set out to homeschool. Or the daughters may take their mothers' questioning of school's assumptions even further by challenging standardized tests, for example, or by deciding not to go to college even though their mothers had always imagined that they would.

I said that homeschooling parents often begin by replicating school in the home and then relax into a much looser setup, with the child teaching herself rather than being taught through formal lessons. As families go through this process of transition, the parents have to learn to trust their children. Over and over again parents write to homeschool journals and speak to one another about this process. And as they learn to trust their children, they in turn learn to trust themselves and their own perceptions.

Often, rather than being a matter of self-sacrifice, homeschooling becomes a way for the mother to discover more about her own goals and to learn what she has always wanted to learn. On an immediate level, this may happen because the mother finds herself learning French or math or history along with her daughter as the two of them explore the world together. On a more abstract level, if a mother raises her daughter to follow her own interests and goals, the daughter may in turn encourage the mother to do the same for herself. I know one homeschooled girl who, having felt her own interests taken so seriously by her mother, then urged her mother to adopt the same attitude toward her own work and went so far as to hang a sign on her mother's door that said, "Do Not Disturb: Writer at Work."

As a single parent wrote to *Growing Without Schooling*, "In being home with my daughter, I'm finding out what it means to create my own life."[33] Similarly, a mother wrote during her family's first year of homeschooling that

> People are often amazed at how "selfless" I am. They think they could never spend so much time with their kids, do all the necessary preparation it must take to "teach" all those subjects, etc. Actually, I have never been so self-indulgent. I always wanted to learn French and take piano lessons and when [my son] asked to do these things, I knew that here was my chance! . . . I am feeling very alive and full.[34]

This is a sentiment many homeschooling mothers feel or, perhaps more accurately, come to feel over time. In chapter 1, I discussed the misconceptions about homeschooling that the girls wish they could address. Homeschooling mothers often have their own list of misconceptions that they believe others hold, and chief among them for many is the idea that homeschooling their children is at odds with their own self-fulfillment.

Some women argue quite rightly that staying at home does not mean failing to work. They may be working for pay from the home, or they may see spending time with their children as important work. They may see their work in terms of the interests they are pursuing and the activities they are involved in, whether or not these are specifically paid jobs. When homeschooling is added to the picture, I believe it often heightens awareness of these ideas, both because logistical considerations necessitate this awareness and because taking their children's interests and pursuits seriously prompts mothers to do the same for themselves.

There are mothers who see themselves as feminists and who view homeschooling as an explicitly feminist choice. These women are almost never recognized in discussions of homeschooling, but their perspectives are important. These excerpts are from letters we received at *Growing Without Schooling* when a reader initiated a discussion of homeschooling and feminism:

I certainly consider myself a feminist homeschooler. That's one of the important reasons my kids aren't in school. At home, the kids can try their hands at anything they've a mind to. They're away from the nasty little games of girls against boys and all the one-upmanship that implies.[35]

I have been a feminist for over twenty years. . . . I've only been a mother and a homeschooler for seven years, so feminism is my natural way and couldn't possibly be separated from my mothering and homeschooling approaches. What does this mean for homeschooling? It really means that my family's overall outlook on life is one of equality and a basic understanding that ability, achievement, and work at home and away from home are not gender based.[36]

My basic view is that neither sex should be limited by stereotyping.[37]

Homeschooling and feminism are very linked for me. I see feminism at least in part as trying to create a sustainable world quite different from the old paradigms. Homeschooling is one very concrete way of helping to create that world.[38]

These mothers talk primarily about how a feminist outlook informs their approach to homeschooling—that is, how it affects what they actually do with their children. Others focused on seeing in a feminist light their decision not to work outside the home.

I am a stay-at-home mother, and have been for the past four years. But I am also very, very much a feminist. In fact, feminism is one of the reasons we are homeschooling.[39]

I consider myself a strong feminist, though I would seem out of place at a feminist meeting where the main concern is getting into the fast lane with all the men and competing with them for power in the corporate world. Of course I support the need for women to achieve status and dignity in the world "out there," but as a stay-at-home homeschooling mom, my feminism takes a different turn.[40]

I have often wondered about the seeming conflict between stay-at-home parenting/homeschooling and feminism, but I am slowly coming to see it as a positive and strong expression of feminism, strength, rights, and the feminine. I have chosen to stay at home and to homeschool—I support choice. I also support equal rights and that applies to everywhere—home, offices, clubs, etc. . . . Feminism means opportunity, self-respect, and pride and that is what homeschooling means to me also.[41]

I said that homeschooling girls often challenge societal norms. Parents who choose homeschooling are challenging a societal norm as well, and just as this can strengthen their children and encourage a healthy resistance in them, so can it be radicalizing for the parents and perhaps especially for the mothers. Homeschooling mothers often write about having to defend themselves against criticism from relatives (sometimes their own parents or husbands). Sometimes they have to stand up to school officials who impose requirements beyond the boundaries of the law. By now, many homeschooling families have lobbied their legislators for better homeschooling laws, and while for some this was probably just one in a long series of activist efforts, for others it was their introduction to the political arena.

A mother reflected on her years of homeschooling after her children had chosen to return to school by saying, "Homeschooling gave me my voice and the language to speak. [It] helped me value being different."[42] This woman has been changed in ways that will stay with her and affect what she goes on to do with her life.

The same was true for Nancy Gruver. In 1992 she came up with the idea of publishing a magazine for girls that would be very different from the children's and teen magazines then available. She wanted a magazine that would take girls' dreams seriously, that would challenge stereotypes and accept girls as they are rather than as the images of the "perfect girl" in fashion magazines tell them they ought to be. She wanted the magazine to be run by girls in addition to being written for girls.[43]

Three years later, *New Moon: The Magazine for Girls and Their Dreams* has a readership of twenty-three thousand and is indeed run by a girls editorial board in collaboration with Nancy Gruver, her husband Joe Kelly, and other adults. When Nancy Gruver tells the story of *New Moon*, she says that one of the things that helped her envision the magazine as a collaborative work by girls and adults was the fact that her daughters had homeschooled for three years, although the magazine does not emphasize homeschooling. The girls had been unhappy in school and had asked to leave. Nancy says that the experience of listening to her girls and taking them seriously and then acting on their wishes by choosing an unconventional path had an important effect on her. It reinforced the idea that she could question and challenge the status quo, particularly when her daughters' needs made such questioning necessary. It taught her that she could do something not universally accepted and could have the courage to explain or even defend herself to others.[44]

Homeschooling, in other words, can give mothers tools for healthy resistance, too. And just as homeschooling can encourage girls to trust their internal authority, making them unusually resistant to external pressure, so can it encourage self-reliance in mothers. Debold, Wilson, and Malave write with concern about mothers' increasing dependence on childrearing experts, saying, "What concerned mother would dare to ignore the kindly advice of well-meaning experts on how to raise a healthy child?"[45] Many homeschooling mothers have done precisely this, especially in the years when homeschooling was less common and less accepted than it is now. These mothers took their kids out of school against the advice of teachers, principals, psychologists, and sometimes their own relatives. They refused to accept labels or prognoses offered about their children, or they refused to believe themselves incapable of doing something experts claimed was solely in a professional domain. It's no wonder that these women then speak in terms of finding their voice or feeling their own power.

HOW DO HOMESCHOOLED girls see their mothers? The girls I interviewed were not the daughters of the specific mothers I've quoted here, but their responses do give a good sense of how homeschooled girls perceive their mothers, particularly when their mothers have chosen not to work outside the home.

Particularly evident is the way in which the girls were able to see their mothers as admirable and doing important work even when they didn't have an income-producing job. Erika, thirteen, wrote, "I admire my mom because she has five kids and I think she's a very strong woman." Kate, fourteen, expressed a view to which many others also alluded. She wrote that she admires her mother for "committing herself to keeping her kids out of school, even though that means a lot more blood, sweat, and toil than the average homemaker has to put up with." Elsewhere, Kate refers to her mother as "a truly great woman" and describes a relationship with her that many adolescent girls would envy. Kate and others like her convey a sense of truly being able to *see* their mothers—to respect their choices, to appreciate their work, and to find them admirable. Often, this means that they are returning the trust and respect that their mothers have given them.

The simple fact of spending so much time together seems to contribute to this attitude of mutual trust and respect, even aside from the subtle emotional dynamics that may also be present. While homeschooling mothers do not need to be constantly involved with their children, and while the girls in this study are often out of the house and involved in their own activities, it is still true that these mothers and teenagers spend more time together than the typical American family does. Corinna, fifteen, wrote, "I think I am much closer to my family than I would be if I was in public school, the main reason being I spend a lot of time with them. I think I'm really lucky to have a good relationship with my parents, and homeschooling has added to the strength of that relationship." Sharon, also fifteen, said of both her parents, "We don't have breakfast, go off to work and school, come back, have dinner, go to bed, you know? We're very open, and we have an open relationship. We talk about a lot of things." These girls feel they know their parents and as well that their parents know them for who they really are.

On the other hand, other girls were chafing against the feeling of spending too much time with their mothers or not being given the kind of independence they wanted. These were the girls who felt less understood, less fully seen and heard. Eleven-year-old Deneen, for example, feels her mother is too overprotective and doesn't let her "do the things I want to do." Deneen would like her mother to let her "do more things," and she would also like to be able to talk to her about boys and about the changes in her body, but she finds it difficult to do so.

Lila, fifteen, describes a relationship with her mother that is, on the one hand, very positive—it's easy for Lila to say "I love you" and "I'm glad you're here for me" to her mother— and, on the other hand, full of the same kind of desire for greater independence and understanding that Deneen describes. Lila says,

> I wish my mom were more relaxed about me. I know she worries endlessly, and I wish she'd realize I am a responsible person and although I might not always make what she feels is the right decision, I will make reasonable choices and I always have my best interest in mind.

Tessa, twelve, also wishes her mother would listen to her and understand her more than she does and—like Deneen and Lila—mentions boys as the most obvious forbidden topic. "I just feel that she's too old-fashioned," Tessa says of her mother,

> and, like, you shouldn't talk back, and I can understand how she feels sometimes, because I babysit, and I can see, you know, like if one of the little kids I babysit for comes up to me and starts talking back to me, I can see, but you know, I'm older now, and I kind of, I don't know, I just feel like I shouldn't have to treat her like some kind of a queen or god. I should be able to talk to her when she talks to me, and not just shut up and say, "Yes, ma'am."

Tessa has a hard time coming up with things that are easy to tell her mother, and the things she mentions are fairly superficial. But "It's hard to talk to her about how I actually feel about some things." Later she elaborates on this:

> I've never been able to talk to her about guys or sex or anything like that, really, and I feel bad about it, I feel like I really want to, because I have a friend who does talk to her mom about everything, and I'm really kind of jealous of that. . . . I really wish I could talk to her about the guys I like, because I know she's been through the same thing, but, you know, I just, somehow I can't, and that kind of disappoints me.

It is perhaps no coincidence that Deneen and Tessa expressed more doubts about homeschooling itself than the other girls did. They were able to list many positive things about it, and they exhibited some of the same strengths (such as an ability to defend themselves even when others held a different opinion) that the other girls did. But their feelings of not being allowed the level of independence they wanted made them see homeschooling as limiting in a sense that the other girls did not.

In a way, Deneen and Tessa were protesting the fact that their mothers were not recognizing the challenging or rebellious aspects of their daughters' personalities: Deneen wants to "do things [her] mother would never *think* of doing," and Tessa wants to be able to talk back, to question. To understand this situation more fully, one would have to interview the mothers as well. To what degree do Deneen's and Tessa's mothers see themselves as resisters? Do they see themselves as challenging society's expectations or standing up for themselves and their children by homeschooling? Perhaps they do. Perhaps the problem is only that their daughters have not yet been able to recognize this in them. Or do the mothers not see themselves as questioning or resisting anything? Perhaps, then, the daughters who see themselves as resisters recognize the discrepancy. A further possibility is that the mothers view themselves as resisters but have not come to terms with their daughters' expressions of their own forms of resistance.

There often seemed to be less tension between a mother and daughter when the daughter perceived her mother as similarly rebellious and skeptical of societal norms. Abby, sixteen, described a very positive relationship with her mother, and said, "We're both sort of rebels. We both tend to go off the beaten track and look at things from a different point of view." When I asked Abby in what ways she herself is a rebel, she answered,

> Well, first of all I'm not in school, which isn't as much of a rebel as it used to be, but it's like, if somebody—I'll just see lots of points of view that everybody starts spouting about, and I'll say wait a minute, I don't agree with that. And I don't mind saying that in front of a crowd. I'll be perfectly happy to get up and say no, I don't think you're right.

Later, when Abby mentioned that she admired her mother and I asked her why, she said, "She's not afraid to say what she thinks." So Abby admires in her mother the same quality she values in herself, and we can imagine that Abby's mother has supported this kind of outspokenness in her daughter throughout Abby's development.

More and more, psychologists and researchers are writing about how crucial this kind of support can be. In an essay called "Raising a Resister," Beverly Jean Smith writes,

> When I read the psychological literature about mother-daughter relationships, mostly what strikes me is daughters' pain, anger, hate, rejection, fear, and struggle to find self. Perhaps these relationships drain some adolescent girls of the energy necessary to resist others' definitional norms.

One good reason to have a healthy, nonadversarial relationship with one's mother is that it enables a daughter to direct her resistance energy toward other things and thereby to preserve her sense of self against others' challenges *and* to make changes in the world around her. Smith is African

American, and she says that although she speaks only from her personal experience, "I know that other African American women and women from different backgrounds share some of what I say." Perhaps the culturally marginal nature of homeschooling allows homeschoolers as well to share some of what Smith says, so that homeschooling mothers, too, are able to support their daughters against "others' definitional norms." I mentioned earlier that many homeschooling mothers have had to resist or ignore the opinions of traditional experts. In fact, many began homeschooling because they supported their children's perspective, took seriously their feelings about school, and ultimately turned to homeschooling as a result. Throughout the process of homeschooling, too, mothers often have to support their children as they grapple with society's expectations regarding academic achievement or social life.

When Smith describes how her mother responded when a kindergarten teacher accused Smith of not playing by the rules, and later when another teacher accused her of lying, she sounds very much like many of the girls I interviewed sounded as they described their mothers:

> Two moments flash through my mind of [my mother] backing up my voice when teachers refused to or just could not hear me. I remember a time when, in kindergarten, I kept telling my teacher I was not sleepy. She kept fussing at me, because I did not take naps. Eventually I told my mother. She came to my kindergarten class and asked the teacher if I got on the cot. "Yes." Did I disturb others? "No." Was I quiet? "Yes." Then she said that was all that could be asked of me. I could not be forced to nap. In fact, even at home I did not take naps, though my sister did. My mother lost half a day's pay. She came to school again when I was in sixth grade, because a teacher kept calling me a liar. I had been questioned by this teacher several times about a fight that had occurred away from the school grounds. She was not my classroom teacher. I reported this questioning to my mother. She always told us to tell the truth and that anything could be dealt with. My sister and I owned up to

all of our actions, good or bad, and faced the music. She assured the teacher that my version of the story was the truth as I knew it. Furthermore, she did not appreciate the teacher calling me a liar and [told her] to quit doing so, since I had explained to her several times that I had told the truth about the incident.[46]

In terms of the benefits of having a mother support her resistance, what Smith got in these situations is probably equivalent to what many homeschooled girls get under parallel circumstances. Though there are often other ways in which homeschooling strengthens a girl's resistance, I'm inclined to think that Smith, while going to school, reaped the same kinds of benefits that a homeschooled girl with the same kind of support now reaps. One difference may be that more homeschooling mothers are generally inclined to support their daughters against others' definitional norms because the need for such support is often the basis for homeschooling. And as the mothers I've quoted have shown, homeschooling often makes resisters out of mothers who had not previously seen themselves this way. It is also clear that support from their mothers is not the only thing that strengthens resistance in homeschooled girls, nor is it always necessary. Other aspects of homeschooling can strengthen a girl's resistance even when her mother is not a rebel or does not explicitly encourage her daughter to resist.

THE HOMESCHOOLED GIRLS who feel supported and understood by their mothers often talk about staying close to them even in the midst of mother-daughter conflict. Eleven-year-old Gita writes, "I can talk about almost anything with her. I love her, I fight with her, I yell at her, she yells at me, we fume away, we come back fifteen minutes later and hug." And Debbie, fourteen, makes a distinction between fighting and "just stating the point." With her mother, she says, she prefers to fight because

With fighting, we raise our voices, and I can say, like, anything, and then she says anything back to me. When you just state a point, you're not mad, so you kind of watch what you're saying and you don't necessarily say what you want to say. . . . I like saying whatever's on your mind and getting it out.

Several of the girls acknowledged their unusually good relationships with their mothers and said they hoped that the openness would continue. Others wished for the chance to talk and to be heard, which they didn't feel they currently had. But no one said, "I'd rather *not* be close to my mother." These girls remind me of what researcher Terri Apter has said about the traditional view of adolescence as a time of separation from one's parents. After interviewing pairs of mothers and daughters, Apter concluded that adolescent girls do indeed want to be recognized as separate individuals and want to be truly seen and understood by their mothers, but they want to maintain connections to their mothers at the same time. They use conflict with their mothers to grow, to understand themselves, and to demand understanding *of* themselves.[47]

Sixteen-year-old Madeline was very aware of the conflicts she and her mother were having and was also equally clear about not wanting those conflicts to be minimized or unexpressed.

As I've been growing up we have more conflicts only because she doesn't want to let me go, and I'm kind of doing my headstrong "I'm out in the world now, it's my turn to be me," and she's like, you know—and especially because I'm young, and she still wants to keep her baby at home. Which I can understand. And—but we have a wonderful relationship. She's my best friend.

Madeline goes on to say that she can tell her mother about anything, "And after she gets over the mother thing," Madeline laughs, "she understands as my friend, too, you know? She's given me a lot of freedom, and we just have a mutual trust of each other."

I ask Madeline if she thinks that the freedom her mother gave her is now in opposition to the way she wants to "keep her baby at home" as Madeline gets older. Madeline doesn't think so.

Her one personality is the liberal, great mother who took me out of school and did all that stuff, and, you know, is letting me do my own thing, and then the other side is the mother, which is like, "Don't leave me," you know, "My baby, I'm worried about you." I just take that—you know, it all goes together. I don't think it conflicts.

Madeline is able to accept her mother's ambivalence and even to laugh affectionately at it, because she is so clear that her mother is not actually stopping her from moving forward and growing up. "No, no, she's just [talking about her fears]," Madeline says, "which I think is neat, because it's important for her to tell me these things, so that she's not pretending to be completely cool when she really isn't."

With a few exceptions, the girls' relationships with their fathers were less close, less mutually respectful, and less interesting than their relationships with their mothers. Whereas homeschooling seems to make possible a very different kind of mother-daughter relationship than is typical, it hasn't yet charted the same kind of territory between fathers and daughters (or fathers and sons, I suspect). Work arrangements have a lot to do with this, though that's not all there is to it. But I say homeschooling hasn't yet charted the same kind of territory because I believe it can and that the few exceptions are proof of this. I see the father's role as not yet as fully explored or as nontraditionally conceived as the mother's, but I also see the potential for this to be the next area of growth or reflection among homeschooling families.

I'll use the few exceptions to illuminate the possibilities. Although this was not the case in the families of any of the girls I interviewed, a handful of homeschooling fathers have chosen to be the ones who forego paid work and stay home to make homeschooling possible. A larger group of fathers have restructured their work in order to be more involved with homeschooling. [48] I know fathers who, feeling left out of all the richness of activity and relationships going on at home, have left their outside jobs for work that can be done from home. Sometimes both parents use homeschooling as the opportunity or excuse to start the home business they have always wanted.

When homeschooling fathers do manage to be around a good bit of the time or when they make a strong effort to be involved and connected when they are around, the effect on their relationships with their children is noticeable. Barbara, thirteen, whose father works outside the home and whose mother does not, nevertheless describes her relationship with her father as a good one, and says, "He is always there when I need him most." In contrast, Sasha's parents both work at home, and yet Sasha still perceives her father as spending more time at work and less with the family, and she says she shares less with him than with her mother.

Nell, sixteen, says her relationship is "different from most father-daughter relationships," and she describes it as "good, close, with lots of humor." She says it's easy to tell her father she loves him, and when she is asked what is hard to say, she thinks for a minute and then tells this story instead:

> Dad came home from a conference once [where] the speaker had said, "Now we're going to talk about taboo subjects, I think you probably learned about taboo subjects when you were little, growing up, because you learned about what you can't talk about in your house." And everybody was nodding yes, yes, yes. Dad came home and said, "Is there anything we don't talk about in our house?" We all thought and thought and couldn't come up with anything. We all know about things we can't talk about in public, things we can't talk about in the workplace, but just—at home, it's, you know, it's pretty much like, there is no limit.

Nell explains that for much of her growing up, her mother and father both worked at home and were both involved in homeschooling and general childcare activities. Of course, this in itself wouldn't necessarily be enough to create a family in which there were no taboo subjects or in which Nell felt close to her father, but it clearly plays a part, especially in contrast to many of the other girls who spoke about not knowing their fathers as well as they knew their mothers simply because they didn't see them as much.

Dana, fifteen, points out that even though her father does have an outside job, "He's home more than most people's fathers," and she goes on to say, "We have a good relationship. I really talk to him." Most striking is Dana's difficulty in thinking of something that she would talk to her mother about but not to her father. She finally says that she might turn to one parent or the other for help with particular academic subjects, depending on which one was better at it and knew more. But with emotional issues, she says that in terms of who would be better to talk to, "It's probably about the same. Probably a lot of people talk to their Mom [more], but I think it's about the same for me, with both of them." And with both parents, Dana can't think of much that is difficult to say or that she wishes she could talk about but feels she can't.

Nell and Dana are, as I said, the exceptions, and they are exceptions not just within the homeschooling community but within the community of teenagers in general. When fathers have made an effort to be involved in homeschooling, both logistically and emotionally, the relationships their daughters describe having with them are closer than the typical teenager's relationship with her father, just as many of the mother-daughter relationships are closer.

Among the girls whose relationships with their fathers were more distant, some had nothing particularly negative to say except that they didn't see their fathers as much as their mothers and didn't know them as well. Some described liking their fathers enough to miss them when they were gone and to wish they could spend more time togther, while others stressed their emotional distance. But in both cases, the bottom line was, "I don't know Dad as well as I know Mom." Hilary, twelve, answered most of my questions about her relationship with her father by referring to the fact that her father worked long hours and she didn't see him much. She said she mostly got along with him when she did see him, but when I asked her how they are alike and how they are different, she concluded, "I'm not around him enough to find out." Her wish for their relationship—and many girls echoed this—was simply that he be around more.

Abby said that "If there's anything I really want to talk to [my father] about, I can," but she too repeated that her relationship with him is "probably not quite as good as [with my mom] because, you know, he's away at work, and he travels a lot with his job, and I don't see him as much." Her father doesn't always know what's going on in her life, not because she feels uncomfortable telling him but just because he isn't around to notice everything. Although Abby couldn't think of anything she would wish for in her relationship with her mother, for her father she wished that he could get the different kind of job that "he keeps trying to find," both because she knows he would be happier that way and because then she and her siblings would get to spend more time with him.

Abby may resent her father less than some other girls resent their fathers because she believes that he would like to be more involved with the family and that it is only the pressure of his job that prevents this. When girls sense that their fathers are keeping an emotional distance, rather than just an unavoidable or unwanted physical distance, they characterize the relationship more negatively. One of the girls described a very close relationship with her mother but said that she has "no communication with [my father] at all" and that their problems intensified when she became a teenager and had to struggle against his restrictions and his worries about her. As typical as these feelings sound—many adolescent girls say these things about their fathers—in this case they stand out more starkly because they are in such contrast to the relationship the girl described having with her mother.

Others talked about wanting to know their fathers better or to hear more about how their fathers felt growing up (two girls discussed this at some length). Their standards for closeness may be higher than other adolescents' because of the closeness they do have with their mothers.

A FEW OF the girls I interviewed were the only child in the family, some were the youngest sibling or in the middle, and many were the family's oldest child,† reflecting the fact that homeschooling is still a young movement and girls of the ages I was studying are still among the oldest in the homeschooling population. It's difficult to make generalizations about the sibling relationships the girls described because they varied so widely and had so many nuances that seemed particular to the individual family. Two very different themes did emerge, however. Several of the girls spoke of being closer to their siblings than is generally thought to be common. They often attributed this to spending more time together and knowing one another better than many schooled teenagers know their siblings and, as in their discussions of their relationships with their mothers, several of the girls said they fought more with their siblings *because* they were more closely involved with them.

The girls who described close relationships with siblings also attributed that closeness to a greater tolerance for friendship with people of varying ages, which is a familiar theme in homeschooling discussions. Thirteen-year-old Barbara wrote about how she is different from her friends who go to school by saying,

> They cannot see why I am so easygoing about playing with younger kids and not saying: "Get out of here little kid." One day I was at my friend's house and her younger brothers were there. They kept saying, "Can we play, too?" [She] said, "No way, get out of here!" And I said, "Why not?" So, finally she gave in, but she still thinks I am different in that way of thinking. However, she still thinks of me as a great friend.

Barbara is the oldest of five children and is no doubt used to accommodating her younger siblings not only in play but

---

† Specifically, four girls were the only child in the family, thirty-one were the oldest child, six were the youngest, and fourteen were in the middle.

as part of their homeschooling activities, so it doesn't automatically occur to her to dismiss her friend's younger siblings. Other girls mentioned distance from siblings as another of the cultural norms or stereotypes that they were resisting. Sixteen-year-old Sonya described how different she and her younger sister were in temperament and interests but said that they had always gotten along very well, especially as young children when they relied primarily on one another for companionship. Sonya writes, "[Other kids] really thought it was weird that I would hug or kiss my sister in public, and wouldn't ever hit or fight with her or even talk bad about her behind her back."

The second theme that emerged was less prevalent but still noteworthy. A few of the girls who were the youngest in their family (or close to the youngest) had older siblings who had *not* homeschooled. These girls mentioned that they sometimes sensed some resentment on the part of their older siblings because the younger, homeschooled one was experiencing more freedom or getting more attention. Thirteen-year-old Kendra is several years younger than her older sisters, and not only is she homeschooling but she is experiencing a more stable family life than her older sisters experienced at her age. Kendra perceives that one of her older sisters, in particular, has some trouble with these differences. "She doesn't agree with it," Kendra says of her sister's attitude toward Kendra's current life. "I know part of her doesn't think I should have the liberation I have, and, you know, be so close to my mother." Kendra goes on to say that

> I think that it's really hard sometimes, because I'm seen as, like, getting everything I want, not because I earned it but because I'm the youngest. Because I have—me and my mother are always together, we're together a lot, really close, so I'm affected by my sisters not always accepting that.

This is, of course, not only a homeschooling issue. When family circumstances change and a younger child reaps the benefits of a more stable home life and more parental attention, many older siblings are bound to resent this. But some of the younger girls were aware that their parents had come to a greater understanding of homeschooling as time went on (either in terms of their approach or even in deciding to homeschool in the first place) and that they were benefiting from their parents' changes. Likewise, several of the girls who were the oldest in their families knew that they were the guinea pigs, the ones on whom each stage of homeschooling was being tested. Some were able to laugh ruefully about this and others seemed to experience it as more of a burden. There were external factors involved as well. Abby, for example, knew that while current regulations prohibited her from playing on certain high school sports teams as a homeschooler, efforts to fight these regulations were underway and the situation might be different for her younger siblings. Some of the fifteen- and sixteen-year-olds mentioned that while there were only a couple of other homeschoolers their age in the vicinity, their younger siblings had many homeschoolers close to their age.

# Chapter 3

## *"We don't have to agree"*

*A* sixteen-year-old homeschooled girl wrote to me:

Everyone sees things differently; it's kind of like people are all
standing in different places, looking at the same scene, but all
seeing something different because they're looking at it from
different angles and heights. Occasionally you find someone
standing in the same place with you who sees generally the same
thing that you do—that's kind of how it is with finding like-
minded people. I guess I'm standing in an unusual place, since I
see things so differently from most people. I like the view from
where I'm standing, though.

"I like the view from where I'm standing," even though it's
an unusual view, even though it's often hard to find others
who are standing in the same place. This comment is representative of the feelings the girls expressed in the interviews:
recognizing their unusual perspectives, trying to find others
who will accept and welcome that perspective, acknowledging
that this can sometimes be difficult, and reminding themselves that their own self-acceptance is paramount.

Even more than they wonder how homeschoolers learn
academic subjects, relatives, neighbors, researchers, and
reporters all wonder how homeschoolers make friends. So
central is schooling to our image of adolescent social life that,
particularly when it comes to teenagers, people assume that
homeschooling must be a trade-off: "OK, maybe you learn
more at home, but you must be a social misfit. After all,
school is where social life happens."

Given the nature of homeschooling in a society where most young people go to school, it is sometimes true that homeschooling removes a teenager from the center of the social action. This is often especially true in small towns where everyone goes to the same school and socializing revolves almost exclusively around school events. A few of the girls I interviewed said they simply didn't see other kids very much, though they had a couple of strong relationships with friends who lived some distance away but whom they saw only occasionally. Whether this kind of isolation actually makes someone a social misfit is open to question, however. Sasha, sixteen, describes the situation of being quite geographically isolated:

I have very few friends that live nearby. My best friend is living in [another state] and I only have one girlfriend who lives nearby, but I haven't seen her in months. . . . I have noticed that whenever I see my friends that are in school, they are glad to see me, but I don't think they think about me as much as I do them. For them they are just seeing someone they don't see very often, but for me, I am seeing the only person my age that I have seen in months.

. . . If I could change one thing [about my homeschooling] it would be to have homeschoolers that are my age and on my wavelength live nearby. My problem all along has been that I don't have anyone that I can relate to. Even when I went to school I didn't feel that I had much (if anything) in common with my classmates. I always felt like an outsider. I have really missed having someone my age that I can talk to about things. It has been really hard on me. . . . I have written to a few people that I know I would be good friends with if we lived near to each other. Don't get me wrong; I do have friends, I just don't have any that I see very often.

Sasha says of herself elsewhere in the interview, "I actually enjoy being different," and goes on to compare herself at sixteen with herself at twelve by saying,

I am more self-assured now than I used to be, and I think home-schooling has had a lot to do with that. [Sasha left school at 12.] Since I don't spend very much time with other people outside of my family, I have had a chance to get my own ideas about things rather than just being one of the crowd.

She also says that at times she has considered going back to school, but she has always decided not to because she doesn't want to give up what she likes about homeschooling.

I always tell [people who ask] that homeschooling is great because you can spend your time learning about things that *you* are interested in, instead of what other people think you should learn. It also gives you a lot of time to think about things like: whether or not college is the best thing for you, and why it is that people put so much importance on name-brand clothes, certain hairstyles, and being in the "in crowd." Best of all you have time to do what you want to do because you're not spending all of your time studying for tests and memorizing things that you will just forget when you have finished the class.

Is it wrong for Sasha to be out of school? Is she suffering from "not having anyone to relate to" in ways that she would not if she had stayed in school? At times, when she feels the loneliness most acutely, she probably wonders if the answer is yes. On the other hand, people who assume that teenagers need other teenagers could learn something from Sasha. If we listen to all of what she says, we can recognize that she has gained from the way she has chosen to live, even if those gains have been at some cost. She has weighed both sides of the question, considered the trade-offs, and made her decision.

I think the question to ask about Sasha and others like her is, how well do they socialize when they have the opportunity? What kinds of friendships is Sasha capable of forming— not how many, but how deep and with how much of her own integrity and sense of self intact? Even when Sasha laments her situation, she never expresses doubt about her actual abilities as a social person. She says she knows that she would be good friends with her pen pals if they lived close by, and she describes herself as "self-assured" and proud of her ability to think her own thoughts. She blames her situation rather than herself for her isolation. A student in school who is socially isolated and who thinks, "No one likes me because I'm ugly/stupid/not cool enough" is worse off, I would argue, than someone like Sasha who thinks, "I like myself but it's hard to find kindred spirits nearby." Sasha trusts her inner voice and her own perceptions. Her ability to understand the structural factors that make things difficult for her rather than to assume she is entirely to blame suggests that she takes the same attitude toward not living up to traditional standards of social life that the homeschooled girls I described in chapter 1 take toward traditional standards of academic life.

Furthermore, Sasha does not simply resign herself to an unchanging situation. She actively works to change it. Six months after I received Sasha's interview I heard from her again, and this time she told me how she has been reaching out to others around the country who have the same interests that she does. She has been invited to write for magazines, to visit pen pals, and to work with adults whom she has met through the mail. Sasha is making a community for herself slowly but surely, and we can even guess that her self-assuredness and the clear goals she has had a chance to develop over the years have helped to make this possible. So these recent events may help her to feel even more certainly that the trade-off was worth it, that it was okay to spend more time alone than most American teenagers do because she got something valuable in exchange.

Some of the girls who were not as geographically isolated as Sasha did mention that when they had occasional doubts about homeschooling, they wondered whether they would "have more friends" or "know more people" if they went to school. This is a legitimate and understandable question, but it is fed in part by stereotypes about teenage social life to which home-schoolers are not immune, and it's difficult to consider the question without also considering the influence of these stereotypes. Just as questions like "Are you up to grade level?" and "Are you learning enough?" can make a homeschooler wonder whether there is some valid external standard by which she ought to be measuring herself, constant questioning about her social life can make her wonder whether she really is a social misfit after all. When almost everyone you meet asks, "But how do you make friends if you don't go to school?" it's hard not to think that perhaps school is the best or even the only way to have a social life. This question ignores the loneliness and isolation many girls experience in school, just as questions about how much homeschoolers learn ignore the academic deficiencies in many high schools. School, being the norm, is not called into question in the same way that homeschooling is, and in both academic and social arenas homeschoolers are asked to reflect on and explain their experience far more than most kids are.

Homeschoolers with good friends who attend school often seem less vulnerable to the worry that if they went to school their social life would improve. These friends give the homeschoolers access to enough of the "typical" social life so that they don't have to feel they're missing out. At the same time, having many friends who go to school often convinces a homeschooler that it is simply a myth that schooled kids are having more fun. Many homeschoolers discover that you don't need to go to school to be friends with kids who do, and that more socializing happens outside school than in it, anyway. One sixteen-year-old girl told *Growing Without Schooling* about having gotten involved with a group of kids from the local high school during the past year, including going to school dances and football games.

> They don't have much time at school to socialize with each other, so it wasn't like I was missing that. They get a 25-minute lunch period, and they have to stand in line and eat during that time.... They never made me feel like an outsider.... [One of them] commented that I wasn't an ordinary teenager, and I tried my hardest to explain to her why I preferred that, but she felt that I had missed out on something. I felt that my brief experience with doing the normal teenage thing more than made up for it.... She was looking at one path and saying, "This is the one you should have been on," and I was saying, "Gee, there's

this path and this path and this path, and here's the one I happened to take, and I'm just as happy with it."[49]

Homeschoolers who know about school's social life mostly through television or movies, on the other hand, are more likely to say that these fictional kids look as though they're having fun so perhaps school really is more fun than homeschooling. Without enough real examples to counter these media images, these homeschoolers are more likely to accept the movie version as the reality.

The girls I interviewed talked about having several friends more commonly than they described themselves as socially isolated, however. A few had primarily homeschoolers for friends, either because they deliberately sought them out (through homeschooling groups) or because many homeschoolers simply happened to live in their area. Most of the girls I spoke with had several friends who went to school, though. Perhaps the most common situation was for the girl to have a few homeschooled friends—sometimes close friends and acquaintances whom she knew through homeschooling groups and activities—and some friends who attend school, whom she met in her neighborhood or through involvement in some kind of community activity.

Since homeschoolers often meet their friends through involvement in a particular group or activity, it's probably more common for them to define their friends according to whether or not they have common interests than it is for school kids, who may be inclined to speak in terms of being in the same class. In this respect, homeschoolers' social life is more like the social life of adults. Homeschooling teenagers meet friends through work and activities that they have chosen for themselves. Depending on the circumstances where they live, they may also meet friends in the neighborhood.

It was common for the girls I interviewed to describe themselves as "different" and "independent," while in the same interview discussing the close friendships they had.

What is truly interesting about homeschoolers' socialization is not the logistical matter of how they meet and cultivate friends but the deeper question of how they maintain those friendships within a context of feeling independent and knowing that they often see things from an unusual perspective. This is the real issue of difference for homeschoolers— not the simple fact of not going to school, but the resulting differences in attitude, feelings about learning, and feelings about oneself.

In their interviews the girls repeatedly stressed valuing the kind of friend who could accept and even celebrate difference. Robin, fifteen, wrote, "I look for someone who has the ability to deal with people that have viewpoints other than their own. Someone with an open mind." Others made similar comments:

> To me, the most important thing in a friend is that they be able to accept you with all your personal peculiarities, mannerisms, opinions, etc. intact. *Yvonne, fifteen*

> I look for someone who has at least a few things in common with me, not including age, race, or gender. I look for someone who can carry on a deep conversation or debate, can stand up and defend their beliefs without worrying about what other people think, will listen to my views even if they don't agree, and who is not obsessed with being popular with their peers. *Kate, fourteen*

> I look for common interests and abilities. Someone that has their own style and is not like everybody else. *Claudia, twelve*

Gabrielle, eleven, speaking about a good friend who went to school, described what had initially attracted them to each other: "She was one of the people who didn't fit with the groups and who didn't seem to worry about it and who encouraged me, too, I guess, to become—to be independent, and to be me."

Critics often accuse homeschoolers of not knowing how to get along with people different from themselves. These quotations suggest that just the opposite is true. Why do homeschoolers so value friends who are different and who will tolerate differences in them? One reason may have to do with the educational philosophy of their families, part of which could be summed up by the words, "Everyone learns in different ways." It's understandable that kids who are used to hearing and repeating this maxim would then be able to extend it to "Everyone thinks in different ways" or simply "Everyone is different, and that's fine."

It's useful for homeschoolers to have developed this attitude because they are continually in the position of explaining their own differences. Claudia, quoted above, wrote, "When I first met some of my friends, they thought [homeschooling] was kind of weird or thought you didn't learn enough. I just said I learn differently than you do." Whether their parents explicitly teach them how to handle such questions or whether they figure it out for themselves, homeschoolers end up learning to stress that they do things differently, or see things differently, and that's okay. Many of the girls I interviewed said that when someone asked them about homeschooling or went so far as to criticize them for doing it, they answered with something like, "I realize that you might not choose it, but it works for me." If pressed, they sometimes went on to defend the actual benefits of homeschooling, but their basic response stressed the idea that people can be different and still be friends.

Self-protection, too, may be part of what inclines homeschoolers to choose friends who respect differences. Knowing that they will be explaining themselves during initial encounters (and sometimes throughout friendships), they need friends who will not dismiss them out of hand for having such an unusual answer to the question, "Where do you go to school?" Whatever insecurities homeschoolers may feel in new situations would naturally make them want to seek out potential friends who are more likely to be accepting of them. It's also likely that homeschoolers simply respect kids who don't define themselves according to "what everyone else does" because they don't define themselves this way either. They value that trait in themselves and like seeing it in others as well.

The only question on which there was almost complete accord among the girls I interviewed was the question, "How important is it to you that your friends agree with you, or you with them?" With one or two exceptions, the girls answered, "Not very important," and went on to explain that agreement was not essential to friendship.

> I don't feel that my friends or people in general should agree with me about everything. I think that being around people with different viewpoints can open your mind to new things and/or help you strengthen and clarify your own position. *Robin, fifteen*

> It's sort of secondary. Me and my friends don't always agree, and most of the time it's fine. Well, of course I'd like them to agree, but there's no way for everybody to, so it can't be very important. *Erika, thirteen*

> It is very nice if they agree with me, but I can't always live my life to please other people, so, although I would prefer if they agree with me, I do stick up for what I believe. *Judy, fourteen*

> I think if you have good friends they won't think you're weird just because you have a different opinion. Speak up, let yourself be heard! *Claudia, twelve*

> If all of us had the same opinions on everything, it would be a boring world. *Lorna, twelve*

> Not very important to me as long as people act like themselves. *Cynthia, fifteen*

> It is not very important to me that my friends agree with me because I'm as independent as most of them are! I just want *me* to agree with me. *Lael, sixteen*

Erika thinks "it can't be very important" for people to agree, because so often they don't. While another girl might find it troubling that she and her friends often disagree, Erika figures that if it happens so commonly, it must be all right. Several of the others I've quoted here seem explicitly to value disagreement rather than just to tolerate it. Abby, sixteen, exemplified this when she said that she looks for a friend "who's not afraid to tell me I have an absolutely stupid idea." Honesty is more important to Abby than agreement, and perhaps she was also echoing Cynthia's sentiment that most of all, she wants people to act like themselves. Since a sense of their own identity is so important to these girls (and I will discuss this further in the next chapter), it follows that they value strong identity in others and don't want friendship to mean that either one has to compromise. As Lael's comment suggests, internal consistency or self-respect is more important than some kind of forced harmony or alignment between friends.

How different are these homeschooled girls from girls in general with respect to this question of disagreement between friends? Recent research into girls' psychology has looked closely at how girls view difference and disagreement. Quotations from some of the girls who have been interviewed and the researchers' comments might suggest that valuing difference and tolerating disagreement is widespread:

> Margaret, a ten year old, observes that "different people have different opinions . . . because you have a different mother and a different family, and a different skin, different color, different eyes, color hair and intelligence." Deb, another fourth grader, says, "all kids have different feelings about different things, so they might disagree." She says it's "good to be different." Difference is apparent, natural, and interesting to young girls.[50]

> They understand that people are different and that difference can be the basis for a real disagreement, but they also experience difference as a part of the life of relationships. . . . Disagreement does not have to jeopardize relationships for these girls. And friends can be friends, even if they have different opinions about someone.[51]

The girls quoted here sound very much like the girls I interviewed, and these researchers' comments sound very much like the comments I've just made. But "these girls" being described here are *young* girls—eight- to ten-year-olds. The writers I've just quoted are contrasting the attitude of these preadolescent girls with the attitude they observed in adolescent girls: "Continuing observations suggest that adolescent and adult women silence themselves or are silenced in relationships rather than risk open conflict and disagreement," write Brown and Gilligan.[52] Speaking of Jessie, a girl they have interviewed repeatedly over several years, they write, "Speaking up about her feelings, no problem at all for Jessie at eight, and of some concern for her at nine, is now, at eleven, the basis for real trepidation."[53] Over and over again Brown and Gilligan quote girls who are torn between wanting to speak up, to say what they feel, and fearing that if they do so they will be excluded or ridiculed. And yet if they don't speak up, they begin to lose awareness of what they really feel and to stop taking their own perceptions seriously. This is what Brown and Gilligan mean when they say that adolescent girls begin to get "out of relationship" with themselves for the sake of relationships with others. Saying what one really feels *and* maintaining friendships begin to seem mutually exclusive. Differences and disagreements become worrisome instead of interesting.

The homeschooled adolescent girls I've quoted, then, sound more like the young girls in other studies, at least with regard to the issue of disagreements and speaking up. "I can't always live my life to please other people," says Judy at fourteen. "Speak up, let yourself be heard!" urges Claudia at twelve. "It can't be very important," says thirteen-year-old Erika of disagreement. Are these girls just immature? Have they not yet lost something that they are inevitably going to lose? This is of course possible, but for now, given what they are saying at thirteen, fourteen, fifteen, and sixteen, it seems more important to ask, why have they been able to *keep* something that is apparently common in girls before adolescence?

BECAUSE THEY PLACE such importance on having their perspective acknowledged and respected, several of the girls I interviewed distinguished between having friends agree with them and having them listen and attempt to understand. Wendy, thirteen, wrote, "I don't really care if you agree with me. Just as long as you respect my opinion you can agree with whoever you want. I would hope that you would give some thought to my opinion, just to look at other sides." Sixteen-year-old Nell said, "It's almost not important at all that they agree with me, but it is very important that they be respectful of my opinions, and if they're not, then it's just [laughs] forget it, I don't want to be around somebody who won't respect me."

In chapter 1, I described Tina, who often has to explain to her friends that she doesn't like getting quizzed and that she learns enough in homeschooling. Tina also finds herself speaking up when she makes choices that are different from her friends' choices:

> *How important is it to you that your friends agree with you, or you with them?*
>
> Not very important. I mean, I like people to see my views, and I like to see other people's views, but you don't always have to have the same opinions. I think it's worse if you do, because you don't have as much of a wide perspective on things, you know—
>
> *How important is it to you that other people agree with you, not necessarily your friends?*
>
> It's not very important to me. As long as people know what I'm thinking, they don't have to listen, as long as they know.

When Tina says "they don't have to listen," it appears that she means that they don't have to agree or act the way she acts as long as they understand what she means and why she has chosen what she has. Later, when asked, "Do you ever defend a point of view that others don't support?" Tina says,

> Yeah, I do. I mean, I try to adjust for the fact—so that they'll understand what I'm talking about, not exactly change their minds, by [my] defending mine, just so that they'll understand it and not be so closed-minded about it.

*What would be an example of a type of thing that you might find yourself defending or explaining?*

Well, I just turned vegetarian a few months ago, and I have to explain that to a lot of my friends, because they're used to us going out to McDonald's and getting cheeseburgers, and I'm like, "Well, gee, I think I'm only going to get a french fries, guys," and they're like, "Oh, well," you know, and they try and put down what I'm doing. And then I try, I defend it, and then I'm like, "I don't care if you agree with it or not, I just want you to understand why I did it, so you don't think it's just like some phase that I'm going through.

Tina doesn't try to talk her friends into being vegetarians, nor does she hide her own vegetarianism from them. Perhaps most important, she doesn't decide that her decision to become a vegetarian will mean that she can no longer spend time with her old friends. For Tina, the goal is to maintain her friendships despite these differences, and as long as she feels that her friends understand her and take her seriously, sustaining the friendships feels possible to her.

For Kendra, being listened to and understood is also very important, and she will call her friends on it if she suspects that they are only pretending to listen. When I asked her what she looks for in a friend, she responded,

I look mostly for someone I can trust, and talk to, not small talk but talk that, like, really makes a difference. Someone who understands me, someone who's like me in some of the same ways, you know, likes to talk a lot about things that—one thing I have a problem with is some of my friends, I'll talk to them about, like, something that really means something to me, or is bothering me, and they don't—they'll say "Yeah, yeah, yeah." And then, like, they start talking about, you know, yesterday, what they did. So I don't have, like—there's a few friends that that happens with and that's really hard.

*What do you do when that happens?*

Sometimes I really want to keep talking about it, and sometimes I will, sometimes I'll say, "You're really not listening to me, are you?" [laughs] and that's what I usually say, and they'll say, "Yes I am, yes I am," but I know that doesn't mean—so I look for someone who really cares about me and what I feel and what I talk about and cares to hear it.

As with Tina, it's interesting to think about the choices that Kendra has in this situation. She could give up and stop trying to tell her friends what is important to her. She could even decide that the problem is within her, that what she has to say isn't interesting enough and that she shouldn't keep trying to find someone who will listen. But instead she describes a strategy that involves first letting her friends know that she realizes they aren't really listening, and second looking for someone who will listen if these friends won't come through.

In her interview, Kendra returns repeatedly to the fact of her unusual perspective on education, on life in general, and her interest in communicating this to others. Like several of the others I've quoted, disagreement is not a problem for Kendra, but dismissal or disrespect *is*.

*How important is it to you that your friends agree with you, or you with them?*

Hmm. It's not very important to me. I mean, we both, we're all different, there are some things that bother me that they don't think alike, you know, like things that really make a difference, like if any of them are prejudiced against black people, things like that really bother me, but, you know, just like, other things that aren't quite so big to me, I don't, it doesn't bother me if they don't agree with everything I say, because they don't, and it doesn't bother me too much. Sometimes it bothers me when they don't *see* what I'm trying to say, so there's no way they can really agree with it, if they don't see my side, my point of view, that bothers me sometimes.

Kendra, at thirteen, has been out of school for three years. The decision to leave school was difficult for her and involved persuading her mother to understand how school felt to her and why she felt she would be better off not going. Once she began homeschooling, she and her mother struggled with pressure from school officials and from relatives (including Kendra's father and sisters). So for Kendra, homeschooling is very bound up with issues of being heard and understood and with making the effort to explain her perspective. When talking about speaking up and defending her point of view later in the interview, Kendra makes it clear that these acts are very important to her and perhaps even a crucial part of the new sense of herself that she has developed in the past few years.

*Do you ever defend a point of view that others don't support?*

Yes, very often, and more lately, and that feels really good, because I say what I feel and not what I think they want to hear. I meet a lot of people through—we travel a lot right now, so I meet a lot of people, and a lot of times, like, [they say] things I disagree with—things about school, things about teenagers, about children, because society always, very often, talks badly about them. So [defending a point of view is] something I enjoy doing because I disagree and I say—so they see, and a lot of times they see, they really see, that things don't have to be, you know, the way that they're often thought of.

*Why does it feel really good to disagree more now?*

Because I feel like I make a difference, and I feel confident in what I'm saying, I feel like I've, you know, I made them see another point of view.

Still later in the interview, Kendra talks about what she would do if people criticized her for homeschooling:

When I think about grown-ups [criticizing me], I picture myself explaining to them, I picture myself fighting, almost, like, really, really disagreeing, you know, and making my point clear.

*Have you actually done that?*

Yes, very much, and it feels good to, because, again, it's a different point of view, and they really don't understand.

Kendra relishes disagreement because she loves the chance to "say what I feel and not what I think they want to hear." Disagreement is a challenge, not a problem.

But even if it's important, speaking up is not always easy, as several of the girls acknowledged. A few of them said that they would speak up even when it was difficult because it was important for the other person to hear what they had to say— sometimes for the other person's sake, sometimes for their own sake. Nell, sixteen, explained her willingness to confront a friend who looked potentially anorexic.

My friend R. and I were worried about [our friend] D. because she was so thin, she was—the collar bones, and her ribs! So we decided that if at the end of two weeks she hadn't, you know, she was looking thinner or whatever, we were going to talk to her and say we're worried, as her friends, and not say, "Are you anorexic?" but say, "Are you feeling all right, are you feeling sick these days?" or whatever. But she went to the doctor for some other reason and she was told to gain weight, and she was told over and over by her mother so she did start gaining some weight, so we didn't go up to her, but we did think about talking to her.

*When you two made the decision to talk to her, were you scared that she might get angry at you for bringing it up?*
I don't know whether R. was. I thought D. might be annoyed, but I'm not close enough friends with D. to think she might be *angry* angry, but I don't know, I suppose she could have been.

*What made you say, Well, we'll do it anyway?*
Well, she was my friend, I—I guess it didn't really occur to me to just stand there, because I know she didn't always listen to her mother. You know mothers are always telling kids, "Oh, I want you to eat more!" And I'm sure D., had she been anorexic, would have been just, you know, "Oh Mom, lay off, lay off."

*So you don't know what R. thought, but it did cross your mind, "D. might get irritated with us."*
Oh yeah. But too bad, I'm talking to her anyway.

Nell was willing to speak up because she cared about what was happening to her friend, even though she admitted that speaking up might have put that relationship at some risk in the short term. "It didn't really occur to me to just stand there," says Nell. For her, the decision to speak up was not even much of a dilemma. I was the one asking Nell to consider whether she was worried about risking her friend's anger; she in turn answered, "I suppose she could have been [angry]," but her voice conveyed that this was not a serious concern, and anyway, even if it had been, "Too bad, I'm talking to her anyway."

Sharon, fourteen, described a difficult situation that she had confronted just weeks before I interviewed her. She had gone shopping with two other girls, one a close friend and the other someone the friend had brought along but whom Sharon didn't know well. When they came out of one of the stores, the two other girls proudly revealed that they had shoplifted some of the clothes, and Sharon, who hadn't known that shoplifting was part of the plan, now had to decide whether to spend the rest of the day with these friends. She was afraid that if she stayed with them and they got caught, she too would be accused of shoplifting, and as she said repeatedly, she resented being put in that position.

Though Sharon did spend the rest of the day with these friends, she later told her mother what had happened, and her mother told the friend's mother, who had been worried that the girl was shoplifting but hadn't been able to confirm her suspicions. Explaining why she decided to tell her mother what had happened, Sharon said,

> Someone was going to have to find out, and, you know, I thought it would be best if I told my mother and my mother told [her mother], rather than [her mother] finding out that she was right by, you know, [my friend] being hauled off to the police station or something.

Then, even though Sharon essentially dispensed with the immediate situation by putting it in her mother's hands, the issue would not be closed for her until she had also confronted her friend.

> I still haven't told [my friend] that I don't want to be with her when she's doing something like that. I don't really care if—well, I do care, I know it's wrong, but if she's going to do that while she's by herself, that's her business, but I don't think it's fair for her to do that when I'm around, because, I mean, if something happened, I could get something like that on my record, and I don't think that's fair. . . . I still need to tell her how I feel and I just haven't really been able to get her alone to tell her.

> *So that's another part of the picture for you. Even though [her mother] knows and that's sort of taken care of, you still feel like you want to talk to [your friend] directly.*

> Right, because I want to tell her that, you know, I don't feel like she should be doing this around me.

> *When you get up the courage to tell her that, do you think you'll also tell her that you told your mother?*

> I don't think I will, because, you know, I don't want her to blow up about that. I think that if [telling her mother is] taken care of, right now she needs to know that I feel that what she did was wrong.

> *What if she does get angry even at that?*

> Well, I think that I'll just tell her—you know, I know that I'm right, and I know that it's her problem and not my problem, and, you know, if she does get angry, then I just won't be going shopping with her until she says that she's not going to do that when I'm around.

The more Sharon talks, the more it becomes clear that it's important to her that her friend know how she feels, independent of the practical considerations involved in wanting to make sure that Sharon won't have to be present the next time her friend shoplifts. "I still need to tell her how I feel" and "She needs to know that I feel what she did was wrong"—these statements attest to Sharon's need to tell, even more than to her friend's need to hear (which may or may not be a real need—Sharon can't know how her friend will react to what she says).

THOUGH HOMESCHOOLING MAY be the most obvious difference between these girls and their friends who go to school, other differences may also arise, as they did for Tina when she became a vegetarian. What happens when friends have disagreements over more volatile issues than homeschooling or vegetarianism (both of which can become pretty volatile themselves)? Madeline, sixteen, talked about maintaining a friendship despite a major disagreement.

> My oldest friend Gina, she was very prolife, on the abortion thing, and I was very prochoice, and we agreed on everything else in the world, we look alike, everything was the same except for this one issue. We tried to talk about it a couple of times, figuring, oh, we're these great friends, and we're going to have this hot debate on it because we're both very strong, and it was awful! It was like—we were both looking at each other: "How can I love this person so much? You are so stupid!" And so—it wasn't important to our friendship that she agreed with me, it was just important that we didn't talk about it. It was really—it wasn't important for our friendship that we agreed on this. And it didn't make me think—because I think of her very highly, and she was brought up on this kind of, that kind of set, very Catholic, very—I don't know, that's the way she believed life was supposed to be, and it didn't make me think she was a lesser person, I just knew that was something about her that wasn't like me, and I could just put [the fact] away, you know, and we didn't need—and she felt the same way about me.

One could say that Madeline and her friend ought to have been able to talk about their views on abortion, but perhaps the point is that they did talk, and having done that once, they didn't need to keep talking. Or maybe the most important point is that both Madeline and Gina knew what the other felt; they weren't hiding or denying their own feelings by choosing not to talk about them. One can "silence one-self" in the deeper, more insidious sense of not speaking up when one really wants to or ought to, or by not even allowing oneself to think what one truly thinks. But one can also silence oneself in the perhaps less harmful sense of simply and freely deciding not to talk about certain things—which is not the same as deciding not to think certain things or refusing to recognize that you and your friend think differently about something. Although Madeline tells the story to illustrate the point that there are some things friends can't talk about, she may be underestimating the significance of the talking that she and Gina did do. Though in the end they decided not to keep dwelling on the issue, they learned that they could be friends with each other despite such a major disagreement ("It wasn't important for our friendship that we agreed on this") and that friends don't need to be alike in every way ("I just knew that was something about her that wasn't like me").

PERHAPS BECAUSE THEY have so many other occasions during which they have to gather the courage to speak up and express a dissenting point of view, some of the conventional "peer pressure" situations seem less traumatic to these home-schooled girls than they are generally thought to be. When Abby, sixteen, described being the only nondrinker at a party of drinkers, she didn't convey a great deal of anxiety over being in that situation and didn't seem to think it was particularly heroic that she had stood her ground in this instance.

*What do you think about when you make choices in general?*

Well, most of the major things, it's like, I already know what I'm going to do.

*How do you know? You just tell yourself?*

Yeah, basically. I mean, it's like, especially in college, I've been— I took two [college] classes this semester, and you know, I made a lot of friends there, and I got invited to some parties and stuff, and there was a lot of drinking going on, and I don't drink, and just about everybody else was, and, you know, there was some pressure put on me, but it was something I felt comfortable not doing. And it wasn't something like, I felt I had to make a big decision there.

*What is that pressure like? People always talk about that—*

It was—well, in the first place, only about half the kids knew how old I was. Most of them thought I was about nineteen or twenty, and that made a big difference [laughs]. But even the ones who knew I was sixteen were, like, offering me beer and wine coolers, and I was just like, "No, I don't drink." They're like, "Are you sure you don't want to try it? Have you ever tried it?" I'm like, "Yeah, I've tried it a couple of times, you know, at home. I don't want to do it." It wasn't real hard pressure. Maybe it would've been if I wasn't so sure of myself.

*What happened when you said no? People always worry that they'll lose their friends . . .*

I don't think anything really happened, they were just like, "OK, you don't drink, fine."

Despite my repeated questions, Abby does not see her refusal to drink as a problem. Others might experience such a party as a tension between the desire to stick by their own beliefs and the fear of being excluded or made fun of, but Abby appears not to see it this way. "I don't think anything really happened," she says, telling me that this was not the dramatic incident I or young adult novels would have made it out to be. We don't know how Abby's friends actually viewed her refusal to drink, but she heard them as saying, "OK, you don't drink, fine," which is the important point. Abby didn't view the situation in terms of possible ridicule or exclusion, and therefore she didn't hear those motives in her friends' responses.

It is because of just these sorts of situations that adults would like girls not to be vulnerable to peer pressure, and it is for just these reasons that the idea of a girl standing up for herself or sticking by her beliefs seems attractive. In other respects, however, the idea of a girl behaving this way is often threatening, and adult women's own ambivalence about this behavior may be part of what makes things difficult for girls. Naomi Wolf, in her affectionate but hard-hitting critique of contemporary feminism, *Fire with Fire*, suggests that women's discomfort with dissent, and with standing apart from the crowd, has ramifications that are political as well as personal. I said earlier that sixteen-year-old Lael did not put an artificial harmony or alignment between herself and other girls above other considerations. Wolf suggests that many women do consider harmony to be their greatest priority and that this stonewalls certain kinds of progress. She argues that women would benefit from being less afraid of dissent and from understanding how to work with others even when they disagree. She says that women can be too inclined "to think of other women's dissent as betrayal, rather than as a difference of opinion," and that this tendency can get in the way of effective action.[54]

If Wolf's charge is accurate, then a greater comfort with disagreement and an ability to maintain friendships or alliances despite disagreement will later make these home-schooled girls an asset to the community of adult women. But in the meantime, women's ambivalence about speaking up and standing alone affects how we respond to girls and how we expect them to act. While adults don't want girls to give in to peer pressure in some instances, we also fear the idea of a girl being isolated or excluded. Yet sometimes a girl needs to risk isolation or exclusion in order to say or stand by what she really believes. Naomi Wolf writes,

> Since girls' social organization is based on cliques, a girl's originality of spirit, which implies dissent from the norms of the group, can put her at risk of social death. . . . Since originality can be penalized by ostracism, girls learn that they must seek safety in consensus; they get little reinforcement from other girls—unless they are very lucky and have found a clique of rebels—for taking an unpopular view, challenging the status quo, or sticking to a conviction in the face of general condemnation.[55]

Since this type of social organization is so firmly fixed in many people's minds as normal for adolescent girls, it's no wonder that "Don't you miss the social life?" is the first question a homeschooled teenager gets asked. Often a simple answer about the various ways in which homeschoolers can meet other kids does not satisfy the person who asked the question, because what is really behind the question is a deeper concern about being "out of it" and not fitting in.

But as true as Wolf's description rings for many of us, it is simply not the case that the social life of all adolescent girls is or has to be centered around cliques. Just as our assumptions about how kids must learn are challenged by kids who are learning in a very different environment, so are our assumptions about adolescents' emotional and social lives challenged by what these homeschooled girls show us. If it is possible to have friends and yet not to have cliques as one's central organizational structure, then cliques are not necessarily natural or inevitable. Critics wonder if adolescents socialized along nontraditional lines will be able to get along in the world; maybe the point is that they will get along in and help to create a different type of world, a world in which dissent is possible, in which one can challenge the status quo and stick to a conviction.

Of course, homeschoolers are not completely invulnerable to pressures to be just like everyone else. But as they wrestle with these pressures and weigh the alternatives, they engage in a kind of self-reflection that gives rise to an important kind of strength (as it does for girls who wrestle with doubts about how they are learning). Ultimately, this reflection can let them see themselves as having chosen the life they are leading, rather than just having been born into it. Sasha engaged in this type of reflection when she thought about what she would lose by going to school and possibly making more friends. Similarly, twelve-year-old Gwen says that each year she considers going to school, and occasionally the idea of being like everyone else seems attractive. When she thought about going to school this most recent time, "Part of me wanted to go to school and say

'Hello everybody! See, I'm normal just like you,' and most of me wanted to stay home." In the end, Gwen says, "I decided going to school wasn't worth it." She says of others who might criticize her for homeschooling that "homeschooling is my life, and if they don't like it, they can eat it." Being normal may be a temptation, but in the end not one that is strong enough to draw her into school. Just as Sasha blamed her situation rather than herself for her isolation, another homeschooler I know once said of her desire to meet more kids that "I don't wish I were in there, but I do wish more of them were out here." This seems to express the feelings of many homeschoolers. They decide that going to school isn't worth giving up what they value about homeschooling or about themselves, but they wouldn't mind having more like-minded people out here with them.

A fourteen-year-old wrote to *Growing Without Schooling* about the tension between wanting to be normal and realizing the costs of thinking in these terms.

> When I was little I used to say, "When I grow up I'm going to be normal. I'm going to have one child who goes to school and we're going to eat junk food and do all the normal American things." In the past two years or so I've really started valuing my individuality, valuing that I am different. I know that teenagers in our society usually want to conform, but for me it's been the opposite: the older I get, the more I want to be different. I see people falling into a pattern of dependency, of wanting to be just like everybody else, and I see the peer pressure in my friends who go to school.[56]

Defying the common pattern, this girl has become more comfortable with herself and with being different from others as she has gotten older. I think a lot of this has to do with the self-reflection I mentioned earlier. As she has gotten old enough to be able to reflect on her situation, she has come to see what she has gained from it. It may also be true that as she has come to an age when many of her friends are suffering exactly the sort of "loss of voice" and of self-esteem that researchers describe, she sees the issue more starkly as the differences between herself and her friends become more apparent.

THERE IS NO doubt something about homeschooling itself that encourages respect for differences, just as there is something about traditional schooling itself that discourages it. One could argue, for example, that cliques are a response to an unnatural situation in which young people are kept with others their own age, secluded from the rest of the world, and dealt with in groups rather than individually. Ironically, though, much of what characterizes homeschooling at this point comes from its being an unusual choice and an unusal perspective. If home-schooling were the norm, the girls I interviewed wouldn't have reported so many incidents of trying to explain themselves to others and being aware of their unusual perspective. Would this then mean that they would be less sensitive to the issue of differences in friendships than they are now? Would their ability to deal with differences be less noteworthy? Much of what is difficult about homeschooling comes from its being a marginal activity, but as I've suggested many of the strengths it engenders come from precisely this marginality.

I am going to describe in chapters 5 and 7 how skillful homeschooled girls seem to be at resisting oppressive cultural norms and challenges to their own identity. Would they be less skillful at this healthy resistance if homeschooling were not itself a form of resistance? Or is there something about homeschooling itself that nourishes healthy resistance, whether or not one is actually resisting anything by home-schooling? One could argue that while school aims to make everyone the same, homeschooling itself, regardless of how common or uncommon it is, has the opposite goal. Perhaps, therefore, if homeschooling were the norm or just more com-mon than it is now, there would be more diversity among people and thus, out of necessity, a greater tolerance of dif-ferences. At this point in the history of homeschooling, these questions cannot be fully answered.

# *Chapter 4*

## *"I like who I am"*

"*I* like how I've learned, I like who I am, and I like what I know." Fourteen-year-old Andi is talking about what she says if people criticize her for homeschooling. Her voice seems to ring with confidence and a slight edge of defiance, as if she is used to explaining who she is and answering to people who try to challenge that. Throughout her interview, she returns repeatedly to the idea that *her* opinion of herself is what matters. When I ask her how she wants to be able to describe herself in ten years, she replies, "Pretty much the same [as I am now]. I like who I am a lot." A few minutes later, I ask if she admires any adult women, and she says that she admires her mother for working hard for what she believes in, but other than that, "I think some women are really great, but there's nothing I really particularly admire about them."

"Do you notice different adult women and think, this is one I'd like to be like?" I'm pursuing the question, still imagining that Andi will be able to say more clearly what traits she admires in adult women and hopes to have for herself. But Andi says, "I've never really compared myself, [saying] this is what I'd like to be like, because I'm going to like to be like whoever I end up being."

Finally I realize that *this* is Andi: this self-acceptance, this awareness of who she is in the world. She is determined to hold onto her good opinion of herself even in a world that sometimes threatens to shake that security. Everything she describes in her interview seems to revolve around this axis of self-respect: her anger at her best friend for betraying her by telling one of her secrets, her wish that her father could see her "more for who I am and not who he wants me to be," her insistence that her stepbrother respect her instead of teasing her and grabbing at her newly developed woman's body. Andi's stories are about keeping herself clear and whole in the midst of relationships with other people. She obviously values other people deeply, and she says, "I think I'm a good friend, I'm very trustworthy, I'm good at cheering people up," but if people won't take her as she is, she wants nothing to do with them.

When she is asked to tell about a difficult choice she has had to make, she tells a riveting story about having to decide whether to physically fight two of her friends. Andi takes a couple of classes at the local high school, so she mixes with other teenagers in a school setting more than most home-schoolers do, and her story is set in this context.

> I'm in a huge fight with a couple of my friends, and one of them wanted to hit—both of them wanted to beat the crap out of me, and I could've stayed there and fought to the death, or I could've just said, listen, you're all being stupid, so there's no point in fighting, I'm walking away. If you want to call me a chicken, you go right ahead, but you're the person that's the chicken, because I'm doing the smart thing. And that's what I ended up doing, just walking away.

> *What were you thinking about as you made that decision?*

> Well, do I want people to think I'm a chicken if I walk away, or do I really care? And so I figured out what I was going to do. It's like, they said if I went right home after school, I was a chicken, so I said, OK, I'll stay after school, but I won't fight. That way, they don't think I'm a chicken, and nobody else does. I ended up having to say, "Listen, you hit me, there's no chance we'll ever be friends, if there's even one now."

Andi admits that she felt scared and confused as she thought about what to do, but she now believes that going home without fighting was the right decision.

I think violence is rather stupid, doesn't solve anything but maybe makes somebody feel better, and then in the long run they end up feeling bad, like, oh my god, I hit this person. . . .

That was the day I found out who my real friends are, but I didn't lose anything I needed, because if they're going to treat me that way, I don't need them, and if they're going to cause problems and say stuff like that, I don't need them. So I didn't lose anything I really needed.

For Andi, losing friends who don't respect her, who put her in untenable positions, is not a real loss. But when she feels a strong bond with the person and senses that they really do care about her, she is willing to stick with them and work things out. She can be forgiving, but not at her own expense. When her best friend hurt her deeply by telling someone else one of Andi's secrets, Andi openly confronted her friend and told her how angry and hurt she was.

I said, "I've done a good job of keeping that [trust], and you haven't." And she just started crying and she said, "Listen, you're right, it was the stupidest thing I've ever done, and if you never forgive me I'll understand." I said, "I forgive you because you're my best friend and I love you, but don't do it again." So that worked out.

*She hasn't done it again?*
Nope.

*I wonder what her motivation was for doing it in the first place.*
She was being pressured by her other friends, which is really hard.

Here Andi seems much more empathetic and forgiving than she was in the fight scene. In this case, she is willing to acknowledge her friend's vulnerability to outside pressures and to let it go as long as her friend admits that she was wrong. Perhaps that was the problem with the other friends who wanted to force Andi to fight—they wouldn't admit that they were wrong to force that choice on her, and perhaps she didn't sense in them the underlying commitment to her that seems to have allowed her to forgive her best friend. Or maybe the difference is that with her best friend's betrayal, Andi knew that she herself had not done anything wrong, whereas her other friends were forcing the difficult choice on her by asking that she lose face or violate her own principles by fighting. Andi was able to frame the problem in another way by asserting that refusing the fight was the smart thing to do rather than the "chicken" thing to do. But she still does not consider people who would put her in such a position real friends.

Andi was willing to risk confrontation and possible loss of friendship in order to stay true to herself. Furthermore, she tells her story in a way that says, "I count. My perceptions matter." Over and over again I heard this self-assurance from the girls I interviewed. Lyn Mikel Brown writes that "for girls, adolescence is a time of particular vulnerability; a point where a girl is encouraged to give over or to disregard or devalue what she feels and thinks—what she knows about the world of relationships—if she is to enter the dominant views of conventional womanhood."[57] If this is true, then Andi and others like her are particularly admirable as they hold fast to their trust in what they know and feel about themselves and others.

GABRIELLE, AT ELEVEN, is completely different from Andi in appearance and manner, yet her sense of herself is in its own way as strong and as well developed. Andi looks very much like an adult woman; Gabrielle still looks like a girl, although she says that in her mind she often feels much older. Andi moves comfortably in the world of school social life, dating, parties. Gabrielle has not entered this world at all; she talks about reading and writing, about staging political debates with her younger brother, and she still sometimes uses the word *play* to refer to what she does with friends. Andi bubbles over with answers to questions from an interviewer she has never met before; she gives the impression of someone who is used to talking openly about her feelings and who already knows how she feels about most of the major emotional issues I raise. It's easy to imagine Andi staying up late with a friend and talking about exactly the things she is talking about with me, an interviewer.

Gabrielle also has a great deal to say, but she is more measured and precise as she thinks about exactly how to express herself. One senses that at this time in her life she is doing a great deal of self-reflection, and she is now taking seriously the opportunity to convey some of this to an interviewer. She often pauses for several seconds before answering a question, but it is not because she doesn't know what to say. When she does speak, it's clear that she has been searching within herself for all the various aspects of the answer. Her sense of the multifaceted nature of emotional issues is extremely keen. Often she begins an answer with, "Well, there are many sides to that," or "Part of me thinks . . . but another part of me thinks . . ."

Even when she is not specifically asked about her perception of herself, Gabrielle often makes reference to some characteristic of her personality. She seems so familiar with herself and with how she operates that when she is answering questions about how she deals with her parents or her friends or how she feels about more external issues, she invariably sets her answers in the context of her particular style and perspective. The following phrases, culled from Gabrielle's answers to questions not specifically about her own identity, give a good picture of what she knows about herself:

> I pick up signals, as I call them, of how other people are feeling, when other kids don't, other people don't. . . . I need people, I'm a people person, I need to interact a lot. . . . I deal in words, and I need to be able to tell somebody, usually, how I feel or what I think. . . . I have a big problem with people who try to control or manipulate me. . . . I guess I find myself usually in the minority party on things.

Like Andi, Gabrielle cares about maintaining relationships with other people without having to give up any of herself. She stresses that she needs people and is sensitive to them, but she also needs to be able to speak her mind and to be free of someone else's control. One of the reasons she is so pleased with her relationship with her mother is that they can tell each other how they feel—and how they feel about each other, too. "She's one of the very few people who I can tell all the reasons why I'm angry at her. But then of course," Gabrielle laughs, "she's one of the few people who tells me all the reasons why she's angry at me back!" There is delight in Gabrielle's voice as she recounts these angry scenes; clearly she takes pleasure in the fact that she and her mother can yell at each other openly. "I never want to get to a point where we can't speak to each other," she says more quietly, recalling the one or two times in the past when she and her mother weren't speaking. She remembers these as very lonely times. Yet because maintaining her sense of self is so important to Gabrielle, it is also important to her to be independent from her parents, to do things on her own. Reflecting on how she has changed in the past couple of years, she says, "I like to do things, increasingly, away from my parents. I still have good relationships with both of them, I like being with them, but I want to be independent, I want to do things that I didn't dare to do before."

When she is actually asked what words she would use to describe herself, Gabrielle says,

> Different, a writer, an outspoken female, intuitive, I would say, stubborn, or persistent, whichever way you like to phrase it [laughs], and I don't know what the proper word is—individualistic, very strongly myself and with a very strong sense of my identity and who I am and who I want to be, not always how I'm going to do it, but ... [also] very impatient and hot-tempered.

Even if I had not been listening for Gabrielle's perception of herself, her words would have made it plain. Like Andi, Gabrielle says, in effect, "I like who I am and I like what I know." In chapter 7, I will look more closely at Gabrielle's efforts to resist challenges to this strong sense of herself.

I ASKED EACH girl, "What words would you use to describe yourself?" The string of adjectives they offered were usually as revealing as Gabrielle's. The girls were realistic observers of their own personalities, able to include traits they were less proud of (like Gabrielle's "impatient" and "hot-tempered") in their descriptions. Yet I was most struck by their unabashed pride in themselves. Given our culture's injunction against outright bragging, particularly by girls, some seemed to hesitate about listing positive attributes so baldly. The girls interviewed in person might begin, "I don't want to sound like I'm bragging, but . . ." and then go on to describe themselves as smart, talented, or funny. The girls who answered in writing did not have to use these disclaimers, however, and they leapt right in:

> Friendly, funny, outgoing, smart. *Gwen, twelve*

> I have a strong personality. Not the bubbly-nice kind, but I know what I think and feel, and I have my beliefs and don't let myself get pushed around. I am strong-minded, I guess you would say. *Claudia, twelve*

> Interesting, friendly, sometimes absent-minded, talented, smart, self-confident, and happy. *Kate, fourteen*

> Hard-worker, achieving, caring. *Rita, thirteen*

> Confident, self-sufficient, social, thinking, socially conscious, happy. *Yvonne, fifteen*

> Independent, confident, caring, ready to try most anything, intelligent, and different. *Wendy, thirteen*

Some of the girls gave longer answers to the question of how they would describe themselves now and at other points in their lives.

> I am a very creative young woman, and I'm serious about my future. I have strong values for myself and my family. I have several close friends, and I enjoy their companionship and support. I always try to be there for them. I am fairly quiet and reserved, but I have my wild moments as well. I am athletic and kind of a health nut. I love reading, writing, and riding bikes. I am very self-motivated and determined to make something of myself. I try to make the most of life.

When I was nine I basically lived for the present, enjoying my friends and the good times I spent with them. I was a little shallow and immature, but I was still fairly serious compared to my friends. I was also an avid writer and reader, even back then.

When I was twelve I was serious and uptight, mature beyond my years.

[In ten years] I want to be someone who is serious about their life and the direction it takes. I want to be happy with whatever I am doing, and surrounded by a supportive group of friends. I want to be creative and fun to be with. *Corinna, fifteen*

I seem introverted or even sullen until you get to know me and then you can't get me to shut up! I'm a quick wit, but I do have a bad habit of getting my laughs at others' expense. I like to volunteer for jobs. I have a good presence and speaking voice. I like to write and read almost anything. I make friends better with just one person at a time. I cannot stand parties and detest small talk.

The only difference I know of [between now and] when I was nine and twelve was that I cared a whole lot more [about] what people thought of me. I don't care very much now. I think that anyone who likes me has to like *me*, not some false image that I put out. *Carla, thirteen*

Several girls included both "independent" and "caring" (or their synonyms) in their descriptions. Rather than see independence in terms of isolation or separation from other people, these girls seem to think that it is natural to be both independent and involved with others.

One can see this in their dreams for the future as well. At sixteen, Nell said,

I would hope that I would be doing work that I really, really loved, and not being yet another one of those people that's just in a job because they're in a job. I just—I would really hope I'd be doing something important to me. And I hope that I would have important people in my life, maybe an important guy or maybe just some semi-important people, but that I would have close friends in my life. And I would hope that I was still close with my family, the way I am [now].

Sonya, sixteen, whose ambitiousness is apparent throughout her responses as she describes her deep commitment to music, describes her dreams for adult life in a way that includes both fulfillment of these ambitions and a deep involvement with other people.

> I'd like to be able to say that I became really, really good at what I do, but that I never distanced myself from people. I'd like to say I still have all the friends I have now. If I was married I'd like to say I'd be a good wife and mother, and if my parents needed me to take care of them I'd do that. I'd like to be very much involved in the community or in church, very much a part of the area where I would live. I'd like to be a friend of children, to help them be good at what they do, to respect them and make it easier for them to be part of the community. I'd like to be someone that people looked up to, that they came to for advice, who wasn't afraid to be on everyone's level. I'd like to have a home or farm or business that people and kids would just like to be at. I'd like to have a place that looked like a day camp or community center, with kids and animals running all over the place and neighbors and friends sitting on the front porch, big down-home meals on the table and an atmosphere of welcomeness everywhere.

Some of the girls took the question "What words would you use to describe yourself" very literally and focused on their physical appearance. Such answers may reflect the ambiguous wording of the question or may suggest a genuine preoccupation with appearance on the part of some of the girls who answered this way. Even these kinds of answers revealed something of the girls' pride in themselves, however. Judy, fourteen, said as part of her physical description, "I wear glasses, and they look good on me," and Meredith, sixteen, described herself (among other things) as "beautiful inside and out," and remembered that at twelve she was "in an in-between stage physically, but I felt beautiful." Given adolescent girls' typical dislike of their physical selves, it is especially striking to hear these girls so unabashedly call themselves beautiful and to feel that beauty coming from their own perceptions of themselves ("I felt beautiful") rather than from the standards of the culture.

It's also striking to hear them mix dreams of beauty with dreams of competence. At eleven, Samantha dreams of a future in which she would have lots of friends, have traveled, and have a good job. As her list gets more specific, she says, "I would like to be very beautiful," and in the next breath she says with a laugh, "Oh, and I would want to be able to do a jumpshot." Why *not* be beautiful and able to shoot a jump-shot too? At eleven, both seem like reasonable dreams to Samantha, and one can only hope that they will seem just as reasonable ten years from now.

Several of the girls included the word *nice* in their discussion of how they would like to be described in the future, but they were often more vivid and expansive in their descriptions of other characteristics, throwing in *nice* as a kind of after-thought. Eleven-year-old Pia began answering the question about how she would like to describe herself in ten or twenty years by saying, "I'd like to be independent and, of course, nice, and [laughs] all things like that, you know, I don't want to be obnoxious, I would—" Here she paused for a minute, and then continued. "I'd like it if people, when they think about me, not only do they think about me as being nice, but I mean, like—well, I don't know really."

"Not only nice but what?" I asked her.

"But—I mean, not like agreeing with everyone, or something like that, but really standing up for what I think and really being able to do things for myself and not being this helpless little thing that sits around and has everything—has everyone do things for her."

As Pia expanded her answer, her voice seemed to gain authority and vehemence. She made it clear that "nice" might be desirable, but it wasn't sufficient. She might not want to be obnoxious, but she didn't want to be so nice that niceness became equated with helplessness, passivity, or silence. Given that so many girls Pia's age seem to feel burdened by the tyranny of the "nice girl" and her expected behavior, it is interesting that Pia is able to see through this. Lyn Brown comments on how the image of the perfect "nice girl" affects the girls she has studied:

> Like other girls her age [eleven], at the edge of adolescence, Jesse shows an emerging propensity to separate what she knows and loves from what she believes she ought to do in order to be seen as cooperative, kind, and good—the kind of girl others, she thinks, want to be with. If she stays with what she wants and says what she thinks, she fears she may be the cause of social chaos, abandoned by others in her undesirable feelings, her imperfection. If she "pretends" or "agrees" and is nice when she does not feel nice, she abandons herself, her thoughts and feelings and becomes, as Jesse says, "not really me."[58]

It is hard to imagine Andi (for example) trying to mold herself into "the kind of girl she thinks others want to be with." Andi only wants to be with people who want to be with the kind of girl she *is*. We can hear this conviction in Claudia's "I know what I think and feel and I have my beliefs and I don't let myself get pushed around" and in Carla's "I think that anyone who likes me has to like *me*, not some false image that I put out" as well.

Debold, Wilson, and Malave, commenting on Brown and Gilligan's discussion of "the tyranny of nice and kind," say,

> Repeatedly warned by mothers and women teachers to be nice, girls begin to lose power in their most important relationships. They begin to suspect that their mothers would love them more if they were not who they are but instead were nicer and kinder, more nearly perfect. They are put in the impossible dilemma of giving up what they know and feel to keep from being abandoned or excluded by their mothers and the other women closest to them. . . . Girls are told in subtle and not-so-subtle ways that their bad feelings, like anger, sadness, or impatience and, too often, their exuberance have no place in the world. The Perfect Girl is always someone else.

Girls begin to act out their loss of power to the Perfect Girl through competition and cruelty. Girls' cliques and backstabbing duplicate the rivalry and competition they see underlying women's relationships within a male-defined world. . . . They act out their anger covertly through increasingly painful games of inclusion and exclusion.[59]

This analysis underscores the point I raised in the previous chapter about the possibility that cliques are not a natural or inevitable form of social organization for adolescent girls but are instead a response to a particular situation and particular feelings. The more power each individual girl feels, and the greater her sense that she does not have to give up any significant part of herself in order to exist in the world of others, the less likely she is to need to organize her social life by "cliques and cruelty." While Debold, Wilson, and Malave are astute in their analysis of the pressure that adult women's attitudes place on adolescent girls, they don't pay much attention to the effect that school itself has on girls' feelings of losing power, giving up what they know and feel, having to act in certain ways. Yet these pressures are significant, and for some girls perhaps especially so, which is why girls who begin homeschooling after years in school can demonstrate a dramatic change in their attitude toward themselves, and why girls who have been out of school for years can seem to be remarkably free of this pressure and this loss. Of course, homeschooled girls do face challenges to their sense of self, and they have to figure out whether and how to resist these challenges, which is the subject of the following chapter. Nevertheless, homeschooling gives them certain kinds of tools that help to make healthy resistance possible.

# Chapter 5

## Acts of Resistance

*"I*'ve gotten a lot braver in the past year," Hilary tells me. Hilary is twelve, with a sturdy, athletic body and long hair. She has homeschooled all her life and been a serious gymnast for most of that time. When she is asked what makes her happiest, she says gymnastics and reading; like so many of the girls I talked to, she doesn't seem to think physical and mental activities belong in separate categories.

Though Hilary was a bit shy about the interview at first, after a few minutes she has warmed up, and the words spill out of her quickly, sometimes punctuated by exclamations or giggles. Much of her conversation revolves around the culture of the gym where she goes several days a week. When Hilary says she has gotten braver in the past year, she is talking about being able to stand up to girls who tease her.

"I used to not be able to handle teasing at all," Hilary remembers.

> When I was on the team they used to tease me like crazy, but in the last year or so, I think it was last year, about, I just stopped caring. I mean, people have told me I'm stupid—a girl on the team [has]—and that's just sort of annoying, and it makes me a little mad, and a little upset later on, but I can just stick up for myself instead of wanting to burst into tears at that moment. . . . It's not the same kind of upset, like I can't take it. I *can* take it, it's just mad tears. Because I don't consider myself stupid.

Even more than she dislikes the humiliation of being made fun of, Hilary resents the idea that the other girls' ideas about her don't correspond to what she knows about herself. As we

talk for a while about the things the other girls say and how
Hilary handles it—like when she chooses to work out to clas-
sical music instead of rock and the other girls sarcastically ask
for ear plugs—Hilary thinks back to the turning point, the
moment when she became someone who would stick up for
herself instead of just letting herself get hurt. "I think it was
when I went to camp," she begins. She gathers speed, and the
story tumbles out:

> I had a really bad incident where someone said I was walking
> down to the pool carrying two towels, mine and another girl's,
> and they blamed me for stealing it. And I got really mad. Furi-
> ous! Because I don't steal. And, you know, my camp counselor
> didn't exactly believe them, but she checked all my suitcases. It
> wasn't in there, but later the girl, she found her towel, so she
> apologized for blaming me, but still—and after that I just felt
> like, why don't I just stick up for myself?

Because Hilary had not actually stolen the towel and
because the other girl apologized for her mistake, this might
not have been such a pivotal incident for Hilary. Someone
else might have brushed it off as an innocent error. But somehow at this point in her life, perhaps because she had been
teased so often in the past and described in ways that didn't
match her own opinion of herself, Hilary decided that this
incident was the last straw. I asked her why she thought it
became so important to her.

> I got really mad. Instead of getting so upset. It's like, I don't
> steal, and I don't want to get blamed for stealing. And it's also
> being accused of lying. I don't like being accused of lying either,
> because, you know, if they say I'm stealing, and I say I'm not
> stealing, and they say well, you did steal, that's like [they're] say-
> ing, "You're lying."

For Hilary, the difference between getting upset and getting mad is the difference between internalizing others'
taunts or accusations, or at least remaining silent about them,
and actively defending herself by insisting, "How you see me
is not the way I am!" This is what so enraged her at the

camp—that she was being accused of doing something that would have violated her own principles and her own perception of herself ("I don't steal").

Hilary not only stuck up for herself by openly denying the accusation; ultimately, she switched to a different cabin for the remaining days of camp. She says that she made the decision to switch by herself. From her report, it appears that the counselor didn't give her much support either in helping her clear her name or in recognizing what a challenge to her identity the whole incident became. Unable to get any support in her old cabin, she switched to another where the counselor liked her and respected her ability to be responsible about camp chores.

Hilary chose to handle this incident in a way that would preserve her self-respect, even though she risked the loss of her peers' approval and doesn't seem to have earned the respect of the original counselor, either. Though the girl apologized for blaming Hilary, she didn't become Hilary's friend, and indeed the girl and her best friend remained tightly bound as a pair and didn't do much to let Hilary in. So Hilary doesn't appear to have gotten much from others in this incident.

What she did get was her self-respect and an ability to handle future situations in a way that would continue to preserve that self-respect. What Hilary remembers is that she stuck up for herself, not that others at the camp actually believed her. Similarly, when she talks about defending herself against her teammates' taunts nowadays, it's not clear that she succeeds in changing these girls' opinion of her. The girl who called Hilary stupid may still see her that way despite Hilary's denials. But what matters to Hilary—what she keeps coming back to—is the change in the way she has been able to handle these kinds of situations. She has changed even if the other girls have not, so the incident at camp goes down in her history as signficant.

At twelve, Hilary is able to describe herself as someone who has several good friends but who does what she believes is right rather than what everyone else is doing. "I don't go with the flow," she explains. When a neighborhood girl asked Hilary why she wasn't interested in dating yet, Hilary was able to make her feelings clear:

> A girl who lives across the creek, she asked me if I wanted to date, and I said no, and she said, "Why not? Because you can't *get* a date?"

> *How did you feel when she was saying those things?*
> A little confused, a little annoyed, and a little embarrassed.

> *Did you say anything back to her?*
> Well, I said no, I don't want to go out, and I wouldn't really care, beause it sounds sort of boring, and I don't have time anyway because I've got gymnastics.

> *Do you have an idea in your head of when you would start dating?*
> Not until I'm in high school, or maybe even later, when I'm in college or something.

Though the neighborhood girl wanted Hilary to think that her not dating was not a choice but was the result of her inability to attract boys, Hilary made it clear that she didn't want to date at twelve, which she reiterated when she explained to me her own idea of when dating would be appropriate.

When girls talk about bravery, they often mean daring to speak up or to demonstrate their skills publicly. Hilary said she thought she was brave for defending herself, and she also referred to famous gymnasts as brave because they worked so hard and were willing to perform in front of others. Similarly, thirteen-year-old Kendra remembered a choice she had to make about whether to be in a dance performance, and she considers herself brave for having dared to try performing for the first time.

For sixteen-year-old Nell, however, the choice was about whether to *stop* performing. Nell had been performing with a ballet company for several years, and very happily, by her own description. When she was fourteen, however, she noticed that she wasn't enjoying performing as much as she had been in previous years. Nell was clearly used to being aware of her own feelings and heeding them, and if other people had not been part of the equation, Nell might very well have stopped performing right then. But at just this time, her ballet teacher told her that she wanted Nell to dance a leading role in the next production.

"I said I have some real concerns about that," Nell recounts, "and so she called me into her office and we had this talk which was not a talk, it was a lecture, and then she ended up basically saying yeah, you're going to do it." Feeling pressured by her teacher's insistence, Nell agreed to perform the role, but in the process she became all the more convinced that performing had lost its appeal for her and that she wanted to give it up and concentrate on taking classes for her own pleasure. She said that after the performance,

> I didn't feel this great sense of joy, whereas I often find that [sense of joy] much more in class. We'll be doing a really fun combination and I'm just doing it for me, I'm not doing it for an audience, and I guess that's probably why I'm not making a career out of dance, because I don't dance for the audience, I dance for me.

Nell knew that other people—including her teacher—did feel joyous after performing, but she now saw clearly that this was not how she felt. Again, if left to her own counsel Nell would probably have made the decision to quit immediately, but because she was aware of other people's feelings, the decision became more difficult.

"I knew how important it was to everybody, how much they enjoyed watching me dance," Nell remembers now. "I liked some of the mothers of the other dancers until I stopped performing, and then they basically treated me like, 'I can't believe you're depriving me of watching you dance,' and I was like, don't you care about *my* feelings?" Nell laughs incredulously at the idea that anyone could think that their interest in seeing her perform would override her own firm desire to stop performing. Meanwhile, her own parents, while not actively pressuring her to keep dancing, were questioning the decision and urging her to make it less rashly. The decision, which was relatively easy and straightforward when Nell thought only of her own feelings, became more complicated when she realized that other people had other ideas. As for many other girls, the choice for Nell became a choice between what she wanted for herself and what other people wanted for her.

And like several of the other girls I talked to, the clearest way for Nell to evaluate this issue was not in terms of the pros and cons of performing but in terms of who was most likely to know what would be right for her to do. When asked if there would be another way to see the decision she had to make, Nell replied, "Other people did see it differently." She paused a minute and then laughed.

> Yeah, but they aren't me, and I made my decision, and they— a lot of people just don't understand it, I think mostly they don't *want* to understand it. But it was me, and I didn't make the decision for them, I made it for me, and it's closed, end of discussion, why do—you know, why do these people keep bringing it up?

For Nell, the greatest puzzle is why people keep asking her if she is sure she made the right decision and why they think she should go by anything other than her own gut feelings in a situation where no one else is truly hurt if she heeds those feelings. It seems natural to Nell that she would know herself well enough to figure out that it was time to stop performing, and she doesn't understand why people keep doubting her or suggesting that they know more about her than she herself knows. "They say things like, 'When you're on stage, I can see how much you love it,'" Nell says, "and I don't understand how they can see that when I'm not feeling it." Other people may think they know Nell better than she knows herself in this instance, but she isn't buying that. If they won't make an effort to understand her reasons, she can't respect their interpretations.

Some people find it hard to understand that Nell made her decision, simply, for herself. "Even my parents can't really understand that I'm just being selfish about this," Nell says now, many months after I first interviewed her. They don't fully understand that she chose to stop doing what she didn't enjoy and to continue doing only what genuinely gave her pleasure. It seems easier to imagine—and I too was ready to think this until I listened very closely—that Nell stopped performing because she was afraid she wasn't good enough or because she was getting too good and didn't know how to handle the success. For many girls, either of these feelings in some form might indeed have led to the same decision. But what leaves Nell so incredulous is the idea that people keep letting these ideas of a possible or idealized Nell—a Nell that is easier to understand—get in the way of the actual Nell for whom this decision is completely appropriate.

IN CHAPTER 3, I described the self-reflection in which many longtime homeschoolers engage as they weigh the possibility of going to school against the idea of remaining a home-schooler. When the parents are the ones who made the original decision to homeschool, the children usually confirm that decision for themselves at some point. But this can be a grad-ual process, a growing understanding of their parents' motives and a feeling of having similar motives themselves. Some homeschoolers may entertain thoughts of school peri-odically (think of Gwen making the decision again each year, for example), and others may never give school serious con-sideration at all. Still others decide to try school, either as part of the process of reconfirming for themselves the deci-sion to homeschool or because they have come to feel that school is now preferable. Regardless of what they ultimately decide, simply being able to choose whether to attend school puts these young people in a very different position from most American teenagers. It's an opportunity for them to think seriously about what kind of person they are and what kind of life they want, and so it's not surprising that several of the girls I interviewed gave this choice as an example of one of the hardest choices they have wrestled with.

A homeschooler confronts the matter of whether to attend school with an awareness of the societal bias in favor of attending. Many people mistakenly believe that homeschooling is all right for the elementary school years but difficult or impossible as one gets older, so as homeschoolers enter adolescence, their relatives, church leaders, mentors, and adult friends are all likely to begin asking the homeschooler whether she is planning to go to junior high or high school. This is also a time when many adult friends imagine they will discover whether homeschooling has actually been the child's own choice all along. So these questions from people outside the family, and sometimes parents' own concerns about whether homeschooling will continue to be feasible, combine with the general social atmosphere in which school is the norm for teenagers, and it's not surprising that many homeschoolers give the question of attending school serious consideration.

When I ask Tina if she has ever had to make a difficult choice, the school/homeschool choice comes to her mind right away. At first she speaks about it in general terms: "It's always been a pressure on me, from people telling me that I should [go], and it's always, in my mind, been a question. I mean, deep in the back of my mind it really hasn't, I've really not considered [it], but outside, I kind of want to, sometimes."

Right away as Tina frames this choice it's clear that the issue is what others think versus what Tina actually feels. I ask Tina if there was ever a specific time when she actually had to make the choice, rather than just consider it briefly, and she tells this story that happened three years ago, when she was twelve:

> My two younger sisters started going to school, and my parents signed me up 'cause I said all right, I'll try it. And then I got there and I had to make the decision whether to go in or not, and I made the decision not to. I was in the hallway, all ready to go, and I made the decision not to.

Many homeschoolers consider going to school, but not many wait until they are actually standing in the school hallway before making the final decision. From Tina's story, it appears that she had doubts about going to school from the moment she agreed to the idea, but she only began to resist the pressures firmly at that final moment.

*What made it a hard choice at the time?*

The fact that my parents had signed me up, bought me all new clothes, had people tutor me, to make sure I was ready, and I was standing there in the hall!

*What were the things pulling you on the other side, the side of not going?*

Well, my own self, my own mind, my own feelings about it, that I didn't really want to be in there and I was really faking that I did, just to go, because a small part of me wanted to. But the biggest part didn't, and that was the biggest thing to me.

Tina right away frames the decision not only in terms of the pros and cons of school itself but in terms of her "own self" versus other people's ideas about what she needed. Even her parents, who had after all been homeschooling parents for years, felt that as long as she had gotten as far as standing in the hallway she ought to go in. But Tina decided in that moment to listen to "the biggest part of [her]," and she told her parents she wasn't going to go. "I said no, and they wouldn't listen to me at first, so finally I just said, 'I'm leaving!' Finally I just left. They were kind of mad at me, but they got over it quickly."

Though Tina says she was very scared at the time, and not sure whether she was doing the right thing, she laughs when she says that her parents quickly got over being angry. When I mention that another girl in that situation might have been worried about making her parents angry, Tina laughs again, the way people do when they are acknowledging an unavoidable truth about themselves. "A lot of people probably would have gone just so as not to cause problems, but I've never been like that. I've always been like, nope, I don't want to do it. This is me, not you."

Once Tina saw the choice that way, she was able to gather the strength to act on her feelings, and as she retells the story she seems to gather the same kind of steam, leaning back in her chair and laughing as she lays the issue out: this is me, not you. That's the point. When I ask her if she ever remembers that moment when she is faced with other choices, she says,

> Yeah, it—every time somebody has tried to pressure me back into going to school, I just remember that moment, where I was just like, it sounded good at the time, but then when it actually came to doing it, I didn't want to. And that was how I truly felt, and if anybody tried to convince me to go, then it was them that wanted me to go, not me.

That was them, not me. This is me, not you. Tina is talking about identity, not about the relative merits of classroom education versus homeschooling. By the time adolescent homeschoolers are making the decision about whether to attend school, many have already developed a strong identity as homeschoolers and have a clear sense of how being out of school affects them. At heart, the choice about whether to attend school is not just about which would be the better experience but about who is making the decision. Is it the girl herself, and if so, who is she? What is she really like? What does she really value? What does she want for herself? And if the answers to those questions are not the answers other people would give or would wish the girl to give, then the decision about whether to go to school becomes more complicated.

When talking about the decision, girls often use language not only about school itself but about their own sense of identity. This isn't surprising, given that often homeschooling is not simply something these young people do, but something with which they come to identify very strongly. Thirteen-year-old Marina, talking about whether she ever defended a point of view that other people don't support, said that she defended homeschooling, vegetarianism, and feminism, and added, "I have to defend all these things because they're me." She is defending not just her beliefs but herself, because she identifies with her beliefs so strongly. Several of the girls who talked about attending school spoke in similar terms. The choice was between doing what they believed was right for themselves and going with what other people believed would be right, just as Nell's choice about dancing was. This can also work the other way: a longtime homeschooler who sincerely wants to go to school may have to challenge her parents' image of her as a homeschooler in order to convice them that school would actually be right for her.

THE SAME ISSUE of identity was at stake for Sonya, though in a very different way from the way it was at stake for Tina. Sonya at sixteen had been out of school her entire life, and she debated going to school for something that she wanted there that she didn't think she could get anywhere else. Yet for Sonya as for Tina, the issue soon stopped being that simple, and it became a matter of who Sonya was and what kind of environment would allow her to continue to flourish as that person. In her written interview she explained the situation at length.

> I have two loves in my life—bluegrass music and basketball. I had already involved myself as deeply as possible in bluegrass. But I was having trouble playing the kind of basketball I wanted. It had to be a team, not just a few friends shooting hoops in the driveway. I wanted good coaches, which is something I've never really had the opportunity of having. I wanted to play with other players who were serious about the sport, who played well. I wanted to be in a situation where I could work and improve, under tough coaches and players who were better than me that I could set a standard on. And I wanted to be part of a team—a group of kids who worked together and played together, talked in the gym together, and had a common goal.

Sonya had already played on community teams, but she knew that the kind of situation she wanted would be more likely to exist at the local high school, since that's where the resources, the tough coaches, and the serious players would all be found. "If the school would have let me join the team without enrolling,'"* Sonya went on,

> I would have done that. I really only wanted to play basketball and nothing else. But according to [the high school athletic association's] rules, I had to be enrolled. So I thought, fine. I'll enroll. I know the bad things about school and I'd always been a dedicated unschooler but I wasn't going to act according to other people's judgments until I found things out for myself. I decided I'd enroll and play basketball, and if I just couldn't stand the academic aspects, I'd just have to quit.

Sonya says that the school was very receptive to her and wanted her on the team, so she was all set to begin that fall.

> I was looking forward to my first day when reality finally hit me. It was probably when I was reading all the pamphlets the counselor gave me about courses and rules and times and grades and schedules. I figured out that after I went to classes and stayed late every day for basketball practice, came home, and did my homework, I wouldn't have any time left for anything but sleep, and not enough of it at that.

Sonya realized she would have to give up the music lessons and festivals that were so important to her and wouldn't have quiet time to think, something she had always valued having. She thought she might be willing to give up some of this, but she wanted to know if she would be able to bring her instrument to school and find time to play. "The principal laughed in my face at that," Sonya recalls. It became clearer to her that she would not be able to live the life she wanted and

---

* Many schools around the country do allow this, though they are often more restrictive about homeschoolers' access to sports teams than about their access to musical groups, theater groups, and academic classes.

attend school at the same time. The decision was very difficult, and Sonya vividly describes feeling as if she were "splitting in half" and being forced to choose between two loves—music and basketball—that she didn't think ought to be mutually exclusive.

Though Sonya's particular situation is distinct, the way she describes her thinking process and the basis upon which she made her decision sounds much like Tina's.

> Everyone was trying to convince me to go or not to go, and I just had to sit myself down and say, "Sonya, do what you want, because only you know what you want to do." . . . I figured if I didn't go, I'd be unhappy, but I'd still be myself. If I went, school would probably squelch the "Sonyaness" in me.

So this is what the decision came down to. Sonya still resents that she couldn't do both of the things she loved. She agreed to play basketball on a YMCA team—as the only girl on a boys' team—and she continues to devote herself to music. But she is also trying to challenge the regulations that insist that students who play on the basketball team must be enrolled full time. Sonya feels she learned from the decision.

> In the process of making myself decide, I realized that I really do control my own life, thoughts, and actions. I really don't do what other people tell me. I could have decided not to go because that's the way my mother and all my homeschooling friends thought, or I could have gone to show them that I didn't care what they thought. But I made myself blank them completely out of my mind. And then I guess I knew that I was such an independent person and in such charge of my life that school really would not be good for me.

Knowing that some people might say that she should simply have endured school for the final couple of years and then concentrated on music for the rest of her life if she wanted to, Sonya says,

> But I am what I do, and to not do it would make me a different person. It sounds corny, but "I play banjo, therefore I am." . . .

I'm nowhere near being as good as I could be, but my whole life is devoted to trying, and that's why I can't stop. I could never go to school and be one of the crowd.

Elsewhere Sonya wrote, "I've always had a strong sense of who I am, but going through the decision of whether or not to go to school made me realize that the person I am is not compatible with school." Thus, for Sonya the school decision was about rediscovering what kind of person she was and deciding not to compromise that person or do something that would devalue her. People who might have tried to persuade Sonya with arguments about the value of school or the feasibility of combining music with basketball were ultimately missing the point.

Fourteen-year-old Meredith's decision about whether to enroll in high school after six years of homeschooling was in part a choice between her own values and other people's—as was Tina's and Sonya's—but Meredith's decision was also complicated by one parent's very clear wish that she go to school. As she explains in her written interview,

My father very much wanted me to go to high school. I was not very clear at all exactly what I wanted. . . . It was a difficult enough decision in the first place, and everybody and his uncle telling me what I ought to do did not help.

I was worried that I would become a typical teenager if I went to school. I didn't really think there was anything wrong with the homeschooling, but everyone around me except my mother and a few other family members were telling me very clearly that for me to "succeed," I would have to go to school. People who had never felt comfortable criticizing homeschooling before seemed to feel that this situation gave them free rein. I also had to think about what I would do if I *didn't* go to school.

Though it is common for homeschoolers to have people outside their immediate family criticize the idea of homeschooling and suggest that school would be preferable, having a parent express these sentiments adds a different kind of pressure. Meredith doesn't live with her father, so in one sense she may have felt the pressure from him in a less immediate way, but in another sense she probably experienced this school choice as one of a series of tensions that young people feel when their parents are divorced and have different ideas about childrearing. Yet Meredith says that the situation did not turn into an explicit struggle between her parents because both considered her old enough to make the decision herself. So she was left to contend with the question of what would be best, knowing, as did Tina and Sonya, that the question she was considering was not merely if she should go to school but whose ideas about herself were correct and if she had the courage to do what she thought was right for herself, even if that went against other people's ideas.

> I was very worried. I was afraid that if I made the wrong choice, everybody would be angry at me and disappointed in me. I made the actual and final decision by taking my dog for a walk, I think because I wanted to really be deciding for myself, by myself, without outside influences. I said to myself, "Okay, here are your choices. You can go to ... high school or you can continue to homeschool." It was very plain and unadorned.
>
> I decided to stay with homeschooling because there was nothing the matter with it, and I didn't feel that there was anything that I *really* wanted that school would give me.

Here Meredith sounds rather like Sonya as she talks about trying to shut out the voices of all the other people and simply make the decision by herself and for herself. When she stripped the question of all the attendant pressures, she could see that she didn't actually feel the need to go to school, so she made the final decision on that basis.

Later Meredith comments, "I think some people would have seen [school] as my opportunity to 'be like everybody else.' But I didn't want to be like everybody else. It still hurts that some people, especially my father, thought that I *ought* to be like everybody else." Small wonder that it still hurts Meredith that her father felt she ought to be someone other than who she was. Even teenagers like Meredith, who are very comfortable being different and don't have the supposedly universal teenage craving for fitting in, still have to struggle with the fact that others often imagine they feel this or think that they ought to.

When asked if she thought she made the right choice, Meredith writes,

> Probably. It is very hard to imagine what these past three years would have been like had I gone to school. My ninth-grade year was very hard, but for reasons that had nothing to do with my education. I don't think I would have been any happier in school; in fact I might have been worse off. Anyway, I mostly like the person I am now, so I guess I made a good choice.

Again, when Meredith talks about whether the choice was right, she talks about who she is now—who she became as a result of the decision—not about the pros and cons of homeschooling or school. I'm sure these pros and cons were part of the equation and Meredith did talk about being happy with homeschooling itself, but it is noteworthy how often the language of identity entered into her discussion as well as into Tina's and Sonya's.

These girls have not "given over" a trust in their own perceptions or looked to external authority for a sense of what would be "correct" for them to do. They do what is right for themselves even when staying true means challenging powerful societal norms ("Teenagers go to high school") or the expectations of the adults around them ("If you stop dancing you'll be letting us down").

It is tempting to become so immersed in the stories these girls tell that their responses and decisions can seem like the obvious—the only—courses of action. Why not stop performing if you no longer enjoy it? Why not protest if someone falsely accuses you of stealing? Why go to school if you so clearly don't want to, regardless of how other people may view the situation? But because the literature about adolescent girls' psychology is so full of stories of girls who make choices according to what others want rather than what they themselves want, we have to realize that the behavior of the girls I have described is not typical. A passage from Debold, Wilson, and Malave gives a good picture of the pressures they and other researchers see most girls facing:

> Incorporating images from magazines, books, and television, from other girls, and from the adults in their lives, girls come to label their vitality, desires, and thoughts as "selfish," "bad," or "wrong." They lose the ability to hold on to the truth of their experience in the face of conflict. They begin to see themselves as others see them, and they orient their thinking and themselves toward others. "Like this year I've changed a lot," seventh-grader Michele announces with pride. "I think of, um, more of what to do to be nice than, um, what I want to do."[60]

Passages like this remind me of the other choices that Tina or Meredith or Nell could have made. Tina could have felt that she was selfish or immature for deciding against going to school at the last minute, after her parents had expected her to go and helped her to prepare. Meredith could have decided that she was just plain wrong for not wanting to be like everyone else and for not taking her father's concerns about her education seriously. Nell could have decided that it was wrong to stop dancing when others wanted her to continue. And so on. They could have responded in these ways, but they didn't. Because the alternative response is apparently so common, their ability to hold onto their own perceptions and do what they truly wanted to do is noteworthy.

The mother in the audience who urged Nell to keep dancing essentially accused her of being selfish for not taking other people's feelings into account. Nell, too, used the word *selfish* to describe her actions, but when she said it the word took on a different tone. The audience member stressed the fact that Nell was depriving other people, and Nell stressed the fact that she was heeding her own feelings. The word *selfish* is actually quite slippery. Does it mean immature, egocentric, not caring about other people? Or can it mean (as Nancy Gruver suggested to me) being oneself, literally self-ish?

As I listened to Nell and the other girls and then pored over the transcripts of their interviews later on, it occurred to me that some people might wonder whether these girls were capable of doing things for others, whether they always focused primarily on their own needs.

A few of the girls I interviewed told choice stories that seemed, at first, different from the ones I have quoted here. Abby told about having to decide between attending her mother's fortieth birthday party and attending an event that was very important to her personally. She chose the birthday party. Judy described having to decide between attending camp with her age mates and getting to do some special activities that were available only to that group or attending the same camp with her best friend, in a younger age group, and missing out on some of those special opportunities. The picture was complicated by the fact that her best friend was unwilling to go to camp unless accompanied by her, so Judy knew that if she chose to go with her own age mates, her best friend wouldn't go to camp at all. Judy chose to go with her best friend.

For these girls, other people's feelings figured prominently in their decision making. Judy's sense of how her best friend would feel if she chose not to go to camp with her was what ultimately swayed her decision. Does this mean she acted counter to the way that Nell or Tina acted? I don't think so. The key issue is whether a compromise of identity or a betrayal of self was at stake. Neither Abby nor Judy nor other girls who spoke of those kinds of choices used the language of identity in their descriptions, and it was apparent from the nature of the choice that the choice itself did not present a challenge to their identity or to their perceptions or beliefs in the way that the other girls' choices did.

It's not simply a matter of how trivial or significant the incident seems. The story of Hilary and the "stolen" towel may not seem to involve large issues in the way that choosing whether or not to go to high school does. But as Hilary described, the real story there was that others' ideas about her did not correspond to her ideas about herself. To agree with them or to fail to defend herself would, I think, be the kind of destructive silencing that Brown and Gilligan describe. Similarly, because Nell truly didn't want to keep performing and did not see herself as someone who got pleasure from performing, it would not have been beneficial to her to let other people sway her decision. When Nell put her own desires ahead of other people's, she was doing so because it was necessary in order to stay true to herself. When Abby overrode her own desire to attend another event in favor of going to her mother's party, and when Judy overrode her desire to attend camp with her age group in order to attend with her best friend, they were not at odds with themselves. In fact, they might well have been acting in accordance with their own sense of themselves. For example, giving relationships a high priority may be very much a part of who Judy is, so that by going to camp with her best friend she was actually acting in accordance with a part of herself that she liked and valued. Had Nell continued performing or had Hilary failed to challenge the claim that she had stolen the towel, the opposite would have been true.

Thinking of their desires and thoughts as bad or wrong, losing the ability to hold onto the truth of their experience in the face of conflict, seeing themselves only as others see them—these are the losses Debold, Wilson, and Malave write about, and neither Nell and Hilary nor Abby and Judy suffered such losses. However, the girls who refuse to compromise or betray themselves are also quite capable of generosity and concern for others. More significant, they are able to have these qualities without suffering because of them.

# Chapter 6

## "A whole different person"

$B$ecause this study is not longitudinal, it doesn't trace the girls' development except as they see it themselves. Yet these reflections can be significant. Many of the twelve-year-olds I interviewed described themselves as happy and outgoing, but many of the fifteen- and sixteen-year-olds looked back on age twelve as a time when they felt more awkward and less happy with themselves than they did at the time of the interview. Of course, these are different individuals, and it may be that these older girls really were more awkward and less sure of themselves at twelve than the girls who were twelve when I interviewed them. Still, the point is that the older girls felt that they had grown and even improved over the years of adolescence.

It may seem natural for young people to prefer their current selves to their younger, more childish version. Little children are usually happy about getting older and look with some disdain at the child in the baby pictures, who might have been cute but didn't know as much and couldn't do as many things. Yet the research to which I have been referring throughout this discussion suggests just the opposite pattern among adolescent girls. Against this backdrop, a fifteen-year-old homeschooler who says she feels more comfortable with herself or more confident than she did three years ago stands out, even though the comment is simple enough. A close look at the homeschooled girls who described in greater depth the changes they experienced over time is even more striking.

Of the girls I interviewed, the ones who described the most significant changes between themselves now and three or four years ago were those who had left school for homeschooling in that time. While it was more common for the longtime homeschoolers to say of their younger selves that "some of my thoughts and feelings were different, but I was still me," those who had only recently begun homeschooling spoke of much more dramatic changes, almost as if the person they were then and the person they are now could hardly be considered the same. Much more had gone on than simply leaving school.

SIXTEEN-YEAR-OLD Alexa is so sure of herself as she defends animal rights and women's equality, so enthusiastic in her descriptions of dancing and composing music, and so clearly at home in her body and in the views she expresses that it is difficult to imagine her as the fearful thirteen-year-old she claims she once was. Yet Alexa has no trouble believing the statistics about girls' self-esteem decreasing with each year of high school. I did not bring up this research; Alexa has already mentioned it herself, and she remarks that she felt herself heading down the same path.

"Seventh grade was when I wasn't free anymore," she explains, referring to the last year she spent in school. "I was silent, basically, and that's because I was insecure about things."

"What does it mean to be insecure?" I ask.

"When you're insecure, you can't live normally," Alexa says. "Or you can't live the way you should. You're living in fear, and you don't want people to see you, you don't want to see anyone, you don't want people to see you looking the way you look, so you have to put on your mask of make-up and clothes."

This is a theme that Alexa returns to often: the images of femininity that are perpetuated through fashion magazines and in other media and the vulnerability that she and her classmates felt in relation to them. "I mean, if you flip through a magazine," she says ruefully, "you can easily think, oh my god, I should be wearing that, or I don't look right, or

I need this. But then it's like, I'll just think, well, boys don't have to [do those things], and they're having a fine time. So why do I have to?"

That Alexa can even ask that question is testimony to how far she has come in three years. She is someone for whom feminist writers have made a real difference. They have helped her rethink how she sees herself and what she believes is possible. When Alexa got out of school and began to discover these writers, they helped her reevaluate the pressures and fears she had felt in seventh grade and contributed to the new sense of self that Alexa was constructing.

When Alexa first left school, she spent her time essentially alone—with these writers, with her music and dancing, but without others her own age. Her pediatrician, concerned about Alexa's social isolation, would ask if she was involved in activities with other teenagers, and Alexa would mumble something about the dance classes she was taking. She didn't admit that she didn't *want* to be with other teenagers. "Towards the end of [my last year in school]," she says now, "all I'd gotten from other kids was pain." She needed that time alone, time to read and discover new ways of thinking, time to develop the talents that are now so important to her. Now, almost three years later, she has begun to seek out friendships again, and she is eager to get involved in groups of young people who care about the things she cares about.

It would be nice if Alexa had felt able to be more up-front about her preference for being alone during those years, and it would be nice if her pediatrician had been able to imagine that she might be benefiting from her period of solitude. It's true, though, that Alexa herself wouldn't have known fully how to explain those benefits at the time. All she knew then was that she needed the solitude. Only three years later can she now describe vividly what it made possible.

The dancer in Alexa evaluates her changes over the past three years in terms of the way her physical self inhabits the world. "The way I physically move, the way I go about doing things, is different [now]," Alexa says, and she doesn't mean that she is more graceful or more pleasing to other people. Rather, she is talking about her relationship to the world she lives in, the street she walks on. "I'd get glimpses of it back then," she says, referring to the freedom she now feels. "Like I can remember once walking this dog down the street, and I was looking at my shadow, and it just felt so free and—you just get a glimpse of, not owning the world but living in the world, being part of it."

This is what Alexa has now, this belief that she can inhabit the world *as Alexa*, not as someone behind a mask of fear or of others' expectations. This is what she could only imagine three years ago; this is what the past three years have given her.

If the dancer in Alexa was able to reflect the changes of the past three years through a change in physical movement, the musician in her managed to chronicle these changes in the lyrics of a song. Alexa began writing "Taxi" when she was thirteen. It begins with a girl standing on the street corner, afraid of the people around her and waiting for a taxi to come and take her away. After that first verse is the chorus:

*Taxi—hey, come give me a ride.*
*Taxi—pull on over and let me inside.*
*Been waiting on the curb forever, it seems,*
*But all the taxi drivers have someone better than me.*

This is a perfect metaphor for the way Alexa felt at thirteen: unable to take control, forced to wait for others to help her yet feeling unworthy of their attention. But by the third verse, the girl in the song realizes that she doesn't have to wait for someone else to drive and rescue her. "I can hop behind the wheel and find my own way on the street," she sings. And in the final chorus, the refrain has changed to a jubilant "No, I don't need a ride." The song is no longer about waiting for someone else to save you but about saving yourself, or about rethinking the whole idea that one needs to be saved at all.

When Alexa speaks about the song, she explains that she had originally wanted to write a song about a girl feeling that

*131*

everyone else was better than she was, that none of the taxi drivers would want her. "I had the idea for that song when I was really little," Alexa remembers. "I felt like, why would anyone like me? Why would someone want me as a girlfriend? I thought no one ever would, I thought that was ridiculous."

That feeling was the original impulse for the song, but by the time Alexa had been out of school for a while and sat down to write it out, her changes made writing that song impossible. She no longer had a song in her head about an unhappy girl who feels that all the taxi drivers have someone better. "Then I got older and I said, 'I can't write that song!'" she recalls with a laugh.

Alexa realized that if she was going to write a taxi song, it would have to have a very different ending. She began to think, "How I could turn that into, but I don't want anyone, I mean, if they don't like me the way I am, then I don't want anybody." She began to write a different song, a song that would chronicle the process that Alexa had been through.

It starts out [that] she just wants to fit into the scenery, but she's still questioning it. . . . And in the second verse it's [that] she's getting more confidence and she wants to take control, but she doesn't have any direction, because the world's not set up to help women do that, so it's easy to fall back into just waiting for someone to help you. And then it's "I thought I wanted to wait forever until my one and only taxi came," but then, "How do I know what I want if I've always been told what I want?"

*What do you think the song means at the end?*
It means I'm free now, from the fear that I had before. Like, I don't need a ride, I can get there on my own, and "I can feel the sun shining on me."

I'm free from the fear I had before, and I know what it is to live in the world, to feel that sense of entitlement and security. This is Alexa at sixteen, and the thirteen-year-old Alexa would hardly recognize her.

KENDRA HAS ALSO changed dramatically in the past three years, the same length of time she has been out of school. At thirteen, Kendra describes herself as "sensitive, trustworthy, active, very outgoing, and very successful, because everything that I really want to achieve, I do." If Kendra can feel this way about herself at thirteen, then it cannot be true that thirteen must be an age of doubt and insecurity, as it was for Alexa. The issue for both girls is the changes they have gone through since leaving school, which are at least in part as a result of leaving. Three years ago, Kendra felt

> very unsure of myself, unimaginative, incapable, stuck, not enough, and I notice, like, I look so much different [now], not just because that was two or three years ago but because, leaving school, the first thing I did was cut my hair. I had really long hair [before], my face was, like, really drawn out, and I didn't feel like I was happy at all. I almost feel like I was in a void, when I think about it, like I just, you know, was in between, unaware.

This was Kendra during her last year of school, and although she might have been unaware of her ability to change things for herself, she was not unaware of how school was affecting her or of her objections to much of what went on there. Whereas Alexa suffered particularly from the nature of school's social life and the preoccupations of her peers, Kendra objected to the way her teacher treated the students and the way she found herself worrying about grades but not really assimilating what she was supposed to be learning. Though Kendra was a good student by traditional standards, she didn't feel the acceptance and recognition that she now thinks is so important.

> I didn't see anybody be, like, appreciated for who they were, and acknowledged, and you were very—they didn't want you to accept yourself, feel good about yourself. And you know, I do now, but then, it was almost like if they knew that you accepted yourself, really cared about yourself, you probably wouldn't be there, you know?

*133*

*How could you tell that they didn't want you to accept yourself? What would they do to give you that feeling?*

They wouldn't *say*, "I don't want you to accept yourself." They would act—like when you would start to feel—I saw sometimes when people would be really excited about things, [teachers would] very easily belittle them and what they were doing, like it's not important. [They gave the message that] you couldn't do the things you wanted to, unless you did what *they* wanted you to. And that's not true at all.

While giving the appearance of being an obedient student, Kendra was quietly developing a critique of the classroom environment and gathering strength to resist it. A student with a different temperament might have turned this critique into belligerence and outward rebellion. Kendra continued to play by the rules and to get good grades until the day she came home and told her mother she couldn't go back to school. Her mother let her stay home for a while but didn't take Kendra's request for more than a temporary vacation seriously until Kendra had a terrible nightmare about being trapped and unable to escape. The next morning she and her mother finally talked openly and at length about the depth of Kendra's feelings and the possibility of homeschooling.

Structural differences between school and homeschooling are partly responsible for Kendra's preferring the latter. From everything she describes about how she learns best, it is clear that she benefits from being in an environment in which she can set the pace and in which she can feel recognized and accepted. It is also clear that she benefits from being able to identify and pursue her own goals, an aspect of homeschooling that I described in chapter 1. She has gone from being someone who feels stuck and incapable to being someone who believes that "everything I really want to achieve, I do."

Yet what may be most responsible for the change in Kendra's perception of herself is the fact that at a crucial juncture she learned that she could take control of her circumstances and change them and, furthermore, that her mother supported her resistance rather than override it. When Kendra speaks of her mother now, she speaks of her as an ally, someone who joined with Kendra in challenging what was expected and believing that another kind of life was possible. Her mother didn't initiate the idea of homeschooling, but Kendra doesn't seem angry that her mother didn't on her own come up with a response to Kendra's unhappiness in school. She doesn't need to resent this, because when Kendra herself suggested a solution, radical though it seemed to the family at the time, her mother didn't dismiss it out of hand.

Similarly, when Kendra was frustrated by the way that the school officials' demands infringed on their homeschooling, she asked her mother to request a different arrangement.* In school, Kendra had been the obedient student who didn't challenge the requirements she objected to. But once she realized that she could ask for freedom and get it by leaving school, she had the courage to push even further and ask that her homeschooling be even freer than it had been at the start.

Kendra remembers that "it was scary for both of us" to challenge the authority of the school officials, and at first she and her mother disagreed about whether it was the right thing to do. But ultimately her mother decided to go out on a limb for Kendra again, as she had when Kendra originally wanted to leave school, and both mother and daughter felt their sense of themselves as resisters strengthened. They are now people who believe that it is right to ask for what they need even when those needs are unconventional. Just as Beverly Jean Smith's mother (in chapter 2) supported her even when that meant challenging the teacher who forced Smith to

---

* In some states, the law requires that homeschoolers have the approval of their local school superintendent. This means that families must negotiate with the superintendent about what sort of paperwork they will provide, whether and how often they will meet to discuss the student's progress, and so on. In Kendra's case, the superintendent had been requiring frequent meetings and a greal deal of paperwork. In asking for a less-stringent arrangement, Kendra and her mother were well within the boundaries of the law, but it *was* necessary for them to speak up and ask for what they wanted.

take naps or the later teacher who called Smith a liar, Kendra's mother supported her daughter even when that meant challenging the authority of the school superintendent.

It is easier to see how mothers can support their daughters' resistance when this means going *in* to school with them to argue with the teacher. Mothers who support their children when they want to leave school get far less support from the general public. Parenting magazines print articles about kids who complain of stomachaches or otherwise resist going to school, and the conventional wisdom is always, "Don't give in. Make them go." No doubt many people would have recommended that Kendra's mother do precisely that when Kendra complained of nightmares and asked to stay home. This attitude comes in part from mistaken notions about the viability of leaving school, and sometimes parents need only learn more about homeschooling itself to let their children try it. Often, however, other emotional issues underlie parents' reluctance to allow kids who are miserable in school to leave it. There is a sense, again encouraged by mainstream thinking about this issue, that parents who give in to their children will be allowing themselves to be manipulated or will be teaching their kids that quitting is not always dishonorable. To these sentiments, Kendra and Alexa offer alternative points of view: Is listening to your daughter and taking her feelings seriously the same as being manipulated, even if after listening hard enough you decide on an unconventional solution? And is quitting always wrong, or might it sometimes be an indication of strength and self-awareness? We tend to have more sympathy for adults who leave abusive personal relationships or jobs that are no longer stimulating than we do for young people who deal with a difficult situation by leaving it. Yet for young people as well as for adults, it can take great strength to leave a known situation and create a new one.

And it is not just the being out that can help. Discovering that one can *decide to get out*—that even a ten- or thirteen-year-old can take what isn't working in her life and change it—is very transformative. As Debold, Wilson, and Malave point out, mothers can, without meaning to, undermine their girls' resistance efforts by implying that nothing can be done, that there is no way to change something that isn't working. "Women, unwittingly, collude in girls' gradual disempowerment in a variety of ways," they write. "When girls complain of unfairness in their lives, their mothers often respond, 'Life's not fair.' While true, the passivity and resignation of this response send girls a clear message that they cannot do anything about what they see."[61] These authors fill their book with examples of how mothers can send a different message. Often, these stories are about mothers who support their daughters as they attempt to make changes in school, as Beverly Jean Smith's mother did. These are valuable efforts that can often lead to important changes. What I am saying here is that leaving school is another kind of change, another way for a girl to improve things for herself *and* offer a critique of the existing system, and as girls confront the possibility of making this change, mothers may support their efforts or may dismiss them with the claim that life isn't fair or that difficult circumstances can only be endured.

WHEN ALEXA AND Kendra were having trouble in school, everything still looked all right on the outside. The inner turmoil that they describe seems not to have been visible to people around them. Debbie, however, showed her struggle in more obvious ways. Debbie is now fourteen. She describes herself as "quiet and shy, around most people, reserved, analytical, funny." She plays the piano and considers science her favorite subject. When Debbie was eleven, her mother took her out of school because she was "shoplifting, drinking, [doing] drugs—all the major stuff you hear about, I was pretty much involved in." Unlike Alexa and Kendra, Debbie herself did not initiate homeschooling. Her mother was the one who decided that she needed to be taken out of the situation that was encouraging her involvement in these activities. In that sense, Debbie's mother had the protective motivation that some other homeschooling parents share: she wanted to shield her daughter from bad influences. In that immediate sense, the effort worked. Debbie now feels herself to be "a whole different person." She is still making peace with the feelings that made drinking and shoplifting attractive to her, but she has come a long way.

Yet to think in conventional and superficial terms about peer pressure and bad influences is to miss the depth and the particular pain of Debbie's story. Yes, Debbie felt pressured to engage in those typical "bad" activities, but not because such pressure is somehow a fact of teenage life. Yes, she benefited from being removed from the situation, but not simply because now the "influences" could no longer reach her. Rather, being out of school allowed Debbie to grow into someone who viewed herself in a different way. She now sees herself as someone who can sustain real, close friendships, and who is worthy of such relationships.

Debbie says that until she was in sixth grade, she had no friends at all. She was the one the other kids teased and humiliated. Finally, in sixth grade she found a group of kids who would accept her if she drank and shoplifted with them. "I don't think anyone can actually understand unless they've been through it," Debbie says now.

> I mean, you might think, oh, yeah, it must be pretty bad to be made fun of. But you think, "But I would never do that." But you have to—when you're constantly picked on, when you're walking down the halls and people are yelling things at you that are really degrading, it's like—it's really hard not to, like, turn to something. I mean, when you have a choice of going through that or being with a group that you think will accept you—I mean, what are you going to choose?

As Debbie speaks, I can hear that her painful memories are still fairly fresh. Though she describes herself as reserved, she is very open with an unfamiliar interviewer. She says that she has been seeing a psychologist, and she gives the impression of someone very familiar with her own emotional history, someone very used to retelling it. And yet she wishes that her mother could truly understand this emotional history and could understand the feelings that motivated her behavior. Of her time in school, she says, "I sometimes wish I could tell [my mother] how that felt to me, how bad it really was." She wishes her mother would understand what the pull was, what drew her to look for acceptance in the only way she thought it was available.

Now Debbie is no longer "involved in druggie stuff" or spending time with kids who are. "People who I haven't seen since school, they don't recognize who I am anymore," she says, and she herself agrees that she is completely different from the girl she was three years ago. But is this just in terms of her appearance and behavior? Debbie also talks about some of the internal changes that have taken place, and it's interesting to think about what is cause and what is effect. On the one hand, she says, after she had been out of school for a while, "I started getting friends again, and that really helped, because then I began to feel better about myself, saying, 'Hey, I have friends,' you know." On the other hand, Debbie also says things that suggest that she had already changed, in herself, before she began making new friends, and this makes sense— otherwise, she might simply have repeated the same pattern. The first real friend she made after leaving school was a girl she had known while in school but who had been only a fair-weather friend—"there for the good times but it was like, forget it for the bad times." By the time this friend called her, Debbie "had already taken big steps forward, which made it a lot easier. . . . It was definitely because of homeschooling," Debbie answers, laughing, when I ask her if it's just a coincidence that she happened to become friends with this girl and others after she had left school. "I mean, I know that if I had never been taken out of school, I would—I mean, who knows where I'd be right now, you know? I would still have very low self-esteem, I probably wouldn't have many friends, I would still be involved in druggie stuff like [I was]."

Because Debbie views herself as having "been taken" out of school, the changes she has undergone don't come from having experienced her own power to change things for herself as they did for Kendra and Alexa. But she did learn that circumstances could change, and she learned that in a different environment and with different assumptions being made about her, she could behave and see herself differently.

Everything is not completely resolved for Debbie at this point. She still wishes her mother could understand her behavior of years ago, and she still feels some residual fears about being accepted by other kids. "Now," she says,

> I wouldn't [get involved with drugs] again to be accepted. That's also because I feel accepted right now. But I still will not say certain things. I will sometimes be very quiet around a group, because I'm afraid that if I say some things they'll start laughing at me behind my back, or even in front of me, you know, because it happened so much [years ago].

Three years of homeschooling can't completely counteract six years of humiliation, but Debbie at least reports a major change in her feelings about herself and a hope for continued improvement.

IN A WAY, these stories pose a more direct challenge to schooling itself than the others I recount in this book because these girls have a real point of comparison and feel themselves to have changed so markedly over time—in ways exactly opposite to the ways that girls who stay in school are reported to change. Unlike the homeschoolers who are only relying on speculation or on their friends' reports, these teenagers have actual, often painful memories to fuel their arguments about how school and homeschooling are different.

The girls themselves were the ones who kept introducing the idea that they had changed over the past three years specifically as a result of leaving school. Because of the way the interview was arranged, I asked the questions in the "Coming of Age" section before I asked the questions that were specifically about homeschooling. Thus, when I first asked the girls how they felt about their current selves and how they felt about themselves three years ago, I was asking in a general sense, making no mention of the difference between going to school and homeschooling. Later, when I asked about homeschooling specifically, I asked girls who had only been out of school for two or three years if they felt differently about themselves now that they were homeschooling. But by the time we got to this part of the interview, each of the girls I have described in this chapter had already told their stories about changing so markedly over time. The questions in the earlier part of the interview had already brought these stories forth, and when I then asked the questions about homeschooling in particular, the girls simply echoed their earlier statements or elaborated on them. It was clear that they themselves saw the connection, that they were convinced of the effects of leaving school.

# Chapter 7

## *"More aware of my femaleness"*

*T*hough I have described the various ways in which the girls I interviewed act as resisters, they are not always conscious of themselves doing so. I might hear a girl say, "I look beautiful the way I am," and note to myself that simply to feel this involves some measure of resistance to the pressures that make many girls feel they must measure themselves by external standards of beauty. I might hear a girl say, "I speak up when I have something to say," and think of the research reporting that many girls begin to silence themselves at this age. But the girl who is expressing this resistance may not be aware of it as such because it has never occurred to her to see the situation in another light.

On the other hand, the girls I described in chapter 5 were very aware that some people wanted them to act in certain ways, and yet they chose to act otherwise. The girls in chapters 1 and 3, who are familiar with popular attitudes toward learning or socialization, nevertheless choose to hold their own attitudes. These girls tend to be more aware of themselves as resisters and are even sometimes proud of that description.

My biggest surprise in doing these interviews was exactly how self-reflective the girls were. They told me how they had chosen to act, and they also let me know that they could have acted differently. They knew an alternate path existed, one involving not only actions but feelings. As I sat in the interviews, I often found myself thinking that the metaphor of the crossroads, developed by Brown and Gilligan, seemed quite apt. I saw how the girls could choose—consciously or unconsciously—the path that Brown and Gilligan have described many girls as taking. They could decide not to speak up when speaking up was threatening to others; they could begin to lose sight of their own goals in the face of goals others held for them; they could stop trusting their own perceptions since those perceptions were often out of sync with others'. Yet over and over again, they showed me that they had found ways to resist these pressures and follow another self-selected path.

AT ELEVEN, GABRIELLE is at that proverbial midpoint between childhood and adulthood. She says, "It feels now like I'm—I've just been caught halfway between being a child and being a grown-up and everything's being redecided and reestablished and challenged." When I ask whether she would call herself a girl or a young woman, she says, "Sometimes I think of myself still as a little girl and sometimes I think of myself definitely as a woman." In the interview with Gabrielle, I feel as if I can almost see her standing at that crossroads. But however much in flux things may feel to Gabrielle, she is not indecisive. She has chosen a path, a way to proceed, and it is the path of greater resistance.

Because I'm intrigued with the idea that everything is being redecided and challenged and with Gabrielle's later remark that something in her value system has changed in the past couple of years, I ask her to give me a feel for what that change involves. After thinking for a moment, she answers,

> One thing that's come up quite clearly—I guess it started when I was about ten, and it's been growing and growing ever since—I'm becoming more aware of my femaleness, I'm becoming more concerned about what is called women's issues, and about—before, I thought of myself as a person, and I didn't think much [about] "male-female." Now, though, that seems—that's becoming very clear to me. . . . I'm starting to wonder—I'm trying to set my priorities, and now there's a new factor in it, the female part, and how important that is, what it means.

143

"What *does* it mean?" I ask, almost hoping that Gabrielle will help me answer the same question for myself. But she laughs and says, "Well, that's the big one, that's the one that I'm trying to decide."

That's "the big one" for most girls and women in our culture. I realize that I cannot expect Gabrielle to answer it simply, especially not while she is still in the earliest stages of exploring it. So I go on to ask her about how her awareness of herself as a girl affects her interactions with people now. She mentions that some of her male friends seem suddenly to have noticed that she is female and to have become more uncomfortable with her. She also says that she is "just beginning to realize that there is a difference in how men and women are treated, professionally, as adults, and I'm starting to think very hard about that," and also that "sometimes it seems I can understand things better now when I see that they come from a woman's point of view."

"So," I ask, "I imagine it's more than one thing, but what are the feelings surrounding this new consciousness?"

"I have a whole tangled bunch of them," Gabrielle replies.

I am excited about my growing up and my changing and my becoming an adult and a woman, and I'm also afraid—afraid of being discriminated against, and just afraid of my feelings and the changes that I don't understand. I'm also very curious about it, as I am about most things, only I'm no longer a casual observer of how—of the differences. Now I'm right in it.

We talk some more about this and about the different ways that adults respond to the physical changes that boys and girls go through. When I ask Gabrielle if she envies boys at all, she says, "In some ways, because it feels like—I don't know if this is correct or not, but it feels sometimes like society at large is more accepting of how boys—of boys' attitudes and whatever about it," and I know from the context of our conversation that the *it* here is essentially sexuality. Gabrielle goes on to say that, in boys, sexuality is "a thing more encouraged in them." While sometimes she does envy that encouragement, "then other times I figure, well, maybe I'm going to be the first one to come along and give them a wake-up call!"

As we continue to talk, Gabrielle says she recognizes that boys may have reason to envy girls as well.

> There are some things that are not allowed so much, or are not good for a woman, that are almost required of a man, to be sort of strong, and to be outspoken, and to be sort of a leader, where often, I think, in a woman that's regarded as a threat. But then also, I guess, while on the one hand it's inconvenient for women who *are* strong and outspoken, it also is [inconvenient] for boys who aren't so strong or would rather be quiet or—I guess it would be better for boys and girls alike if it wasn't expected that all boys or all girls would be one sort of thing.

With this statement I realize that we are up against the crucial question of what Gabrielle's awareness of women's issues means *for her.* She has said she understands that women in general face discrimination, but this is vague, not so immediate, and not so specific to her particular personality. When she tells me that society doesn't allow women to be strong and outspoken or sees these traits as threatening, she is telling me about something that hits very close to home. After all, Gabrielle described herself (in chapter 4) as "different, a writer, an outspoken female, intuitive, stubborn, persistant . . . individualistic, very strongly myself and with a very strong sense of my identity and who I am and who I want to be . . . very impatient and hot-tempered." If a girl with a strong sense of her own identity describes herself in exactly the terms that she knows society regards as threatening, what is she going to do about it? Is Gabrielle standing in front of "the wall" that Brown and Gilligan refer to, the wall of a culture that won't welcome her outspokenness, her exuberance, and her temper? Is she going to respond to that confrontation in the way that so many girls appear to, by shutting down, giving over her trust in herself, quieting that outspokenness?

Thinking that only time will reveal the answers to these questions, I almost keep from saying anything about them.

But finally I am too curious to know how Gabrielle perceives the dilemma now, when she is halfway between girl and woman, so I go ahead and ask her what she plans to do about the issue that she has just raised when she looks ahead to the next few years. If she has just explained that society regards outspoken women as threatening, and if she has described herself as outspoken, what does she think will happen to her as she grows up?

Gabrielle's answer lets me know that I need not have hesitated to ask the question, because she has already asked it of herself:

> I am going to remain outspoken. I guess that's one thing I'm sure of, that I'm not going to let what people think I ought to be influence what I'm going to be, any more than— well, I guess if it's really important to other people and not so much to me, but the important things, the stuff that makes me me, if society doesn't like it, well, tough luck, I guess! [laughs] They'll have to learn to cope with it, because I'm going to be me, or—I've tried sometimes to hide what I am and to change it, and I've been miserable. I'm not going to do it.

She says this quietly, but with definite resolve. She is aware of the direct consequences of her actions, and she knows that "the stuff that makes me me" is not going to change, because the alternative in untenable.

"It's interesting," I say to her, "that even perceiving some of the pressures on women, as you do, you can say, 'I'm not going to do that.'"

"No," she says again.

> Because while I may have trouble with that and I might have some negative feelings about that, it's going to be much worse if I try to hide what I am, because I've tried it and I don't think I could really survive much, at least not mentally, if I had to pretend to be something that I was not. I've been able to do it temporarily but if I had to for [longer], I couldn't do it. So I may as well not try to force myself.

This is Gabrielle at the crossroads, seeing two paths and choosing the one that may give her trouble but will allow her to survive with the traits she values in herself intact. In some ways it is less obvious that homeschooled girls would be skillful at resisting these kinds of pressures than it is that they would be good at handling pressures that have to do with home-schooling specifically. Questions about whether homeschooling is the right thing to do are questions that homeschoolers have to answer again and again—they go with the trade, so to speak. But there's no immediate reason why homeschoolers would see themselves as also resisting traditional assumptions about femininity. Nor is resisting these assumptions an explicit goal of homeschooling. As I said in chapter 2, some parents are even surprised when their homeschoolers' resistance takes this form. Once again it seems that as girls develop the ability to resist certain kinds of challenges or pressures, they carry this ability over into other arenas. Once they have learned to say, "I am me, and if they don't like it, they can eat it," they continue to say that even when the issue is not explicitly home-schooling. And as Sasha wrote, "Once you question one aspect of society, you begin to question all of it," and homeschooling can become a crack in the established structure that then calls the rest of the building into question.

LIKE GABRIELLE, TWELVE-YEAR-OLD Hilary is clearly aware of how society begins to view girls as they enter adolescence. She hovers in this same "in between" stage where Gabrielle hovers, still liking to run around and play pretend games but also beginning to develop a woman's body. She is aware that other people's expectations of her are beginning to change. When I ask her if she envies boys at all, she says,

> Well, when you're about this age, some people think that now, because you're a girl, you should be all grown up, you don't run around anymore. But boys seem to get to run around forever! . . . A lot of people think girls should be wearing make-up, and—so that's one of the reasons.

"So how do you feel about all that?" I ask. "Are you going to start acting like that?"

"Not until I want to."

This consciousness of the narrowing of life that can happen as girls' bodies start to change is common among girls Hilary's age, just as Gabrielle's awareness of the perception of women's outspokenness was common. Debold, Wilson, and Malave write,

> Girls' most traumatic loss is the ability to live fully and powerfully in their bodies. Most girls view the physical changes—the complete alteration of the body's shape—not as an empowering experience but as a loss of control. The power that girls gain to reproduce life is typically viewed, by boys and girls, as a curse, not as an awesome mystery. Boys, generally, are excited by the changes in their bodies because these changes give them access to greater control and power in the world.[62]

And it's not just a loss of control that girls can experience, but a feeling of constriction, of having to curtail their activities, as Hilary expressed when she said that boys "seem to get to run around forever" but that girls approaching adolescence are told not to run around anymore. Judy, fourteen, made the same point.

> I wish people would not expect girls to act like young ladies all the time, while boys are allowed to act—they act a lot more freely, they aren't expected to act like gentlemen all the time. Well, girls are, they're expected to act like ladies. And, you know, girls don't always *feel* like ladies all the time. And yet we have so much criticism placed on us when we don't act like young ladies. It's really sad. I mean, if we're supposed to act so kind and, you know, behave ourselves, then why aren't boys?

Yet, when answering the question about how she and her friends feel about their bodies' changing, she said,

I think they and I kind of feel a sense of pride in being women. It changes—I mean, when you get to be a young woman, you feel great, because you know that you're growing up, you have to look toward the future, you have to make a decision about college, you have to make a decision about high school, you have to make decisions when you get older.... There's kind of a pride of being a teenager, of knowing that you are old enough to matter. You can help make decisions in your church, when you get to be my age—I don't do that very much, but yet still, you're getting to be old enough, you can participate in church, you can help out, you can do things more, and I really, I know that I feel a great sense of pride in being a young woman, and I know my friends do.

Judy is eloquent in her protestations but just as eloquent in her celebration of the changes puberty brings. So, as aware as Judy is of the pressure on girls to "act so kind and behave ourselves," she balances this with a pride in being a woman and an excitement that she is now "old enough to matter." Clearly she does not feel completely powerless or limited.

Eleven-year-old Deneen, on the other hand, was unequivocally negative about her body's changes. "I don't like it because I feel like I have to act different," she said, and gave a clue to why she felt this way when asked if she envied boys. She agreed emphatically and said, "Boys are more free, they can do more things." Deneen mentioned several times throughout her interview that her mother was overprotective and that Deneen felt she "couldn't do the things [she] want[ed] to do." Most strikingly among the girls I interviewed, Deneen expressed the more common view of puberty as confining and disorienting, and it seems that her sense of not being allowed to move out in the world to the extent that she wants contributes to this. Whereas Judy speaks of "being old enough to matter" and many of the other girls referred to increasing independence, Deneen seems not yet to have won that right or to be able to see it as an advantage of getting older. It is something she and her mother are still struggling over.

More of the girls I interviewed were positive about puberty or saw it as potentially limiting but were trying to resist those limitations, as Hilary is. In Hilary's case it is possible to see how homeschooling helps her with this resistance; when I asked her if she planned to stop running around (i.e., playing outside, roughhousing), she said, "Not until I want to," making it clear that her own timetable and not society's would be the guide. Hilary was this way about dating as well.

Hilary's homeschooling facilitates this independent attitude in two ways. Homeschooling encourages a general acceptance of the idea that developmental milestones can be reached at a variety of ages. Hilary already knows that kids learn to read at different ages, that she herself didn't learn about fractions when other kids did although she was ahead of them in other areas, and so on. Thus, it is perhaps more imaginable to her that she can decide when she will "stop running around" or begin dating, regardless of what other kids happen to be doing.

I have seen this acceptance of varying developmental schedules manifest itself in other contexts as well. In the older homeschoolers' discussion group, a thirteen-year-old girl explained her feeling that she wasn't yet ready to date, and a sixteen-year-old listener said, "Good for you," even though she herself dated frequently and felt that it was an important part of her life. As I listened to the conversation, I inwardly blanched at the idea of the younger girl's risking embarrassment by admitting to the older girl that she wasn't yet ready to date. I had underestimated the extent to which the older girl would be able to applaud the younger one for doing what she felt was right for herself. (This is another example of the way in which these homeschooled girls are often more comfortable with disagreement and difference than their parents or adult friends are. What I thought might be an awkward moment turned out to be a respectful exchange.)

Also, because she is homeschooling, Hilary is not immersed in the traditional social milieu (although she does indeed have friends), and this may insulate her somewhat from the general pressure to date, even though she is not free of it entirely. She is not surrounded every day with girls who expect her to date—the encounter with the neighbor girl was an isolated incident—and, as I discussed in chapter 5, she has individual friends but doesn't see herself as defined by a clique of friends who set the standards for her behavior.

ABBY, SIXTEEN, IS another one of the girls who has had to struggle with an awareness of the ways that a woman's body can feel limiting. Abby describes herself and her mother as "both sort of rebels. We both tend to go off the beaten track and look at things from a different point of view." She was the girl in chapter 3 who liked a friend "who's not afraid to tell me I have an absolutely stupid idea," and the one who had no trouble not drinking at a party of drinkers. Throughout her interview, in these and other ways, she presents herself as up-front, straightforward, and able to handle being different in all kinds of situations. When assigned to give a talk for a 4-H speech contest about why teenagers should not drop out of school, Abby instead wrote a speech about why kids should consider leaving school. Abby is not afraid to rock the boat, and she feels that she has a competitive streak that not many girls share. Like Sonya (in chapter 2), she has played on sports teams where she was the only girl.

But for Abby, integrating her sense of herself as a girl with her simultaneous desire to be "one of the guys" has at times been difficult. She remembers that at first she hated when she and her friends went through puberty.

"I could always play sports just as well as [the boys] could," Abby says of her childhood years, "and then I guess I hit about—it was really when I hit fourteen, I started realizing I couldn't run as fast, couldn't jump as high, couldn't hit as hard, that kind of stuff." Since Abby valued these abilities, it was hard for her to see any advantages in being a girl or in developing a woman's body. "But then I started getting adjusted to it," she concludes. "Now I like being a girl."

I want to explore how much of that adjustment is simply resignation and how much is genuine acceptance, so I ask Abby more about other people's responses to her as she got older. She recalls that when she was a member of an otherwise all-male soccer team,

> They used to call me a stud, which was a big compliment from thirteen-year-old guys. It wasn't meant in a nasty sense, it was meant as a compliment. And now they wouldn't dream of calling me that. And you know, I guess, guys started paying attention to me, like, as a girl instead of as a—I guess like more as a girlfriend than as a friend who was a girl.

"How did you feel about that?" I ask her.

"I don't know," she answers. "See, a lot of my best friends are still guys, and sometimes people don't understand that." In a sense, Abby has not had to give anything up—she can still have the friendships she had when she was younger. And in some ways, she still feels able to be as competitive as she ever was.

> When I'm actually on the field, I'm still competitive. [This change] doesn't mean I'm any less competitive, it just means, you know, I won't—I mean, it used to be, if somebody started something, I would be perfectly happy to get into a fight with them, and I won't do that anymore. I look for nonphysical ways to get around things.

She laughs. Yet when I ask again if she feels it's possible to have the same kinds of friendships as she had with boys before, she says this time, "Yeah, but not to the same extent, you know, because a lot of guys, you get up to this age and they get a lot of teasing if [they hang around with girls]."

So Abby's assessment of the situation seems to swing back and forth. Sometimes she maintains that she hasn't lost much; other times she admits that she has indeed lost something. This is the area in which Abby finds it hardest to be the way she wants to be or to maintain her sense of herself as she gets older—in other areas it is easier to be a rebel. To anyone else,

Abby looks like a girl who has not succumbed to the stereotype of femininity. She is outspoken, not afraid to go out on a limb for her beliefs, not afraid to be physically competitive with boys. But she knows that growing into a woman has been difficult in some respects. For her, it's the physical aspect that has been most difficult; unlike Gabrielle, Abby doesn't seem to worry about not being allowed to be outspoken, and she tells the story about the 4-H assignment with glee. She is saying that adjusting to some of the new ways that she is perceived and perceives herself has been challenging.

The girls who were most positive about the changes of puberty saw those changes in terms of their own personal (and not just physical) growth or as evidence of a connection with other women. Thirteen-year-old Wendy, for example, wrote, "I see myself a lot differently now. I see myself as a confident person as I am becoming a woman." Judy called her first menstruation "a personal badge of honor," and Lael, fifteen, wrote simply, "I am happy with my body and I love it." Corinna, also fifteen, wrote, "I see myself as more mature, more aware of who I am and what I want. I also see myself as having a connection to women everywhere— something special that we share."

Debold, Wilson, and Malave say that most girls view puberty as a burden rather than as something to celebrate. A friend of mine reminded me that some girls very much look forward to puberty but because they believe it will give them the body they are supposed to have—the body that society values. Both of these attitudes differ from the girls I've just quoted, who celebrate puberty because it positively affects how *they* feel about themselves.

One of the surprises for me, in girls' responses to the question "How do you feel about your body changing, or having changed?" was how many girls felt simply fine about those changes—neither excited nor unhappy, but just fairly neutral. "It hasn't been a very traumatic thing at all," wrote Kate, fourteen. "I don't feel awkward or out of place, and I don't mind all the changes I'm going through. . . . My body may have changed, and along with it a few emotions, but under-neath I'm still the original Kate." Nell said, "I view it more as a slow-changing, rather than this very fast tadpole-frog thing." And yet she too was aware that other people expected her to view her body's changes in a particular way.

> I just didn't think of it as anything really big. I mean, the outside world, when you start maturing and developing and things like that, they—it's like, we live in a society that's so crazed by, oh, you're going to be dating now, you're going to be doing this. And I always just felt like, I have time, it's in the future, you know? But people in the outside world definitely started to jump—oh, do you have a boyfriend? It didn't matter whether it was important to me or not. It was important to them.

Several of the girls echoed these sentiments, and they reminded me that although adults tend to speak as though girls "blossom into women overnight," the girls themselves often experience the changes as more gradual—either annoy-ingly so, in the sense that they feel that it is taking forever to grow up, or pleasantly, in that they feel they have time to get used to the changes. As Nell explains, puberty can be another way in which others' perceptions of girls don't correspond to their perception of themselves.

Madeline experienced the physical changes as more sudden, more "tadpole-frog," than Nell did, but she shared Nell's sense that she was not always being perceived accurately. Now sixteen, Madeline remembers when she was thirteen:

> Well, I went through a very big physical change. I mean, I used to be a little fat kid, you know, and then all of a sudden I was just completely different, and that was kind of weird, just, you know, not seeing myself as this chunky kid anymore but starting to get a woman's body.

*How did that make you feel about yourself?*

Well, it made me feel good after I finally just grew up and lost all the baby fat, that was really nice, because it had always been a struggle for me that I was pudgy, and all of a sudden it was like, yeah, I don't have to worry about this anymore, and that was really nice, it made me feel much more attractive—which made me a little more confident, I think, as you always [feel] if you feel more attractive.

That was kind of a weird time in my life because I kind of blossomed, anyway, and it was really hard for me for a while to deal with, being completely different and people coming up to me and saying, "Oh my god, you've changed so much." Part of me felt like, well, what was wrong with me before, you know? Was I not attractive before, and all of a sudden now I am?

As Madeline has grown older, she has become more comfortable with herself as a young woman, and this manifests itself both in her interest in other young women as potential friends and in her ability to be herself around men. She says,

I went through a stage when I didn't have any girl friends, and I thought men were much more interesting. They were my favorite people to be around, and I wanted to be friends with more men than women, not so much to date them but just be friends.

*What do you think you meant by that?*

I don't know what it was I envied about them, there was something, something just nice about them, that they could be rough, and I felt they didn't have quite as much stigma attached to them. But now actually I feel completely different about it. I prefer women now. I still like men in relationships and I have many men friends, but I've started to gravitate to women as friends more, and I'm finding that it's more and more important in my life to have female relationships, which is very different. I guess I've become more of a tomboy in my older age [laughs], which is interesting. I've decided that I can be rough and do those things too, which I think is what I envied in boys. So I've just kind of become more relaxed in myself.

. . . I think it was [also] that I got more relaxed around men. I started finding that I didn't have to always be something else— or, you know, not that I ever really was [that], but there was always that kind of feeling, when I was learning how to be around men, and now I'm—they call me one of the guys, they joke around with me. But, you know, I'm really comfortable with just being who I am. . . . I kind of just stopped worrying about that kind of stuff.

That's part of, just, getting older, it's like—not worrying about, you know, looking good or that kind of thing.

Madeline is saying that she feels freer now, that she has less of a sense of having to give anything up in order to have male friends *or* female friends. She has resolved exactly the dilemma that Gabrielle and Hilary were facing about whether it was possible to "be rough" and still be an attractive girl and whether she would "have to always be something else" or could be "comfortable with just being who I am." While many girls in other research describe the process of going from thirteen to sixteen as the process of learning how to be someone different from who they were before or how to act in different ways, Madeline describes the process as one of learning that she could be herself and still be involved with boys and men. While the twelve- or thirteen-year-old Madeline felt less relaxed, less able to be rough, the sixteen-year-old Madeline is saying that it is possible to be all these ways without worrying about anything. If we had seen her three or four years ago we might have seen her at the same kind of crossroads at which Gabrielle and Hilary find themselves. Madeline has come out the winner, and Gabrielle and Hilary are determined to do the same. As some of the other girls show, this is one of the areas in which it is most difficult to be a resister, so girls need all the help they can get. I think the experience they have with resisting other kinds of pressures and maintaining their sense of self in other contexts will be part of that help.

# Chapter 8

## Bringing Resistance into School

Until Gabrielle was eight, she went to school to participate in some of the activities there. She always thought of herself as a homeschooler who went into school part-time rather than as a school child who spent some of her time at home, and in this she was like other homeschoolers who take a class or two at the local school or participate in an extra-curricular activity. It's more common for homeschoolers to do this at the high school level, since high school more readily lends itself to part-time participation; it's easier to go in to a high school chemistry class than to try to go into elementary school for science, since the elementary school day is not always divided up into distinct periods or taught by different teachers. Similarly, extracurricular activities in high school are usually distinct and take place at specified times of the day (often after regular school hours). But some homeschoolers do experiment with going to elementary school part-time. For Gabrielle at eight and for other homeschoolers who go into school at older ages, an important issue is to what degree can they bring with them the resistance to cultural stereotypes and the strong sense of themselves that they have been developing as homeschoolers.

Gabrielle remembers how sex-role stereotypes seemed to be rigidly enforced in school. She brought this up on her own as a way of answering my question about whether she herself had actually felt pressure not to be so outspoken or not to be a leader. I had asked her whether she had experienced this pressure directly (as opposed to just hearing about it or anticipating it), and in response she said, "I *have* felt the, you know, 'You're supposed to let the men be the ones who organize or lead or whatever.' And I have been with some boys who take advantage of that: 'Hey girl, *we* are doing this, *we* are organizing this, *we* are fixing this. And then I say, 'Oh no, you're not!'" She laughed and then continued,

> That especially was a problem for me at school. I think a lot of the sort of general stereotypes, at least for me, were more visible there. The boys—there were certain things that the boys did and the girls didn't do. However, I did the things that the boys did sometimes. I built with the Legos, I climbed all the things, I— and then I especially had trouble with the "We boys are doing this, no girls allowed." More than once I got into a fight on the playground.

I asked Gabrielle if the adults at school helped her when she tried to challenge the boys' rules.

> I think often they [dismissed it with] "Boys will be boys." I remember, I went over and complained once because the boys were monopolizing a lot of the equipment and saying, "No girls allowed," and [the teachers] said, "Well, go and play with the other girls," and they went back to chatting. [I said] "But I don't want to." "Go off, we have something else that we're doing." I thought very seriously about getting into a fight with them, too, but I thought that that would just make everything a little bit harder.

Clearly the adults missed an important opportunity here, and I don't think it can be fully understood by saying that they were busy and had many children to attend to, as teachers' limitations can sometimes very justifiably be excused. At the very least, it would have been easy enough to say to Gabrielle, "That's not fair," or, "That's silly; of course you can use the playground equipment." With a little more effort they could have gone over to the playground equipment and talked to the boys, or encouraged Gabrielle to do that herself. Gabrielle did indeed bring her resistance into school, but she didn't get support for it from the adults there, and if she hadn't been able to get that support elsewhere, she might not have been able to maintain and develop it as well as she has.

Why did Gabrielle try to do the things that boys did in the first place? Why didn't she simply absorb the implicit mandates of sex-role stereotypes, as many girls do? Surely part of the reason is that Gabrielle simply wasn't like that; she *liked* playing with Legos and climbing on the playground equipment. But of course she could have liked those activities and yet stopped engaging in them when the boys told her she couldn't. At eight, Gabrielle hadn't yet come to the conscious resolve that she told me about in the interview, the one in which she promised herself not to betray herself or act like someone else. I don't think she was consciously saying to herself, "I will play with Legos no matter what anyone says."

It's probable that because she didn't see herself as fully a member of the school culture, she didn't accept its mandates or assumptions fully either. This is one reason why homeschoolers who go into school are sometimes better able to resist its pressures than the students who are there all the time. Knowing in a visceral way that school is not the whole world, that school's ways are not the only ways, they have a basis for questioning what goes on there or for not automatically assuming that they have to adapt every part of themselves to fit it.

They also, of course, have the chance to get other messages and to experience other ways of doing things during the time they are not in school, and the more they actually identify as homeschoolers, the more this is likely to be true. If Gabrielle in her homeschooling environment was strongly encouraged to follow and trust in her own interests and preferences, she would not be so quick to abandon her preference for Legos even though boys discouraged her. Furthermore, if her mother supported her preferences, she would have an ally of the sort that Debold, Wilson, and Malave repeatedly say is so important. Often, homeschooling mothers whose children go into school only briefly or temporarily become the sort of ally that Beverly Jean Smith's mother was (see chapter 2), because they see themselves at least as equal partners with the school and are sometimes quite willing to support their child even when that means challenging school officials or customs.

Because we were in the midst of discussing so many things at the time that Gabrielle told me about the incident at school, and because I was so struck by her account of the way the teachers had handled it, I neglected to ask her how her mother had responded to that incident and others like it. Later I realized that it was important to know this, so I wrote to ask Gabrielle. She responded:

> One very important thing [my mother] did was to listen to me. I just wanted a sympathetic audience sometimes, and Mama would listen and didn't say that the people couldn't be all that bad. She would listen to my complaints about the girls not accepting me because I was too tomboyish and the boys not accepting me because I was a girl. Often I felt better just having told Mama about it.
>
> She also reassured me that girls could be just as intelligent, strong, fast, etc. as boys, and that they certainly could play with Legos and do other things that I had been told "girls never did." She told me that was a wrong idea that they had, and that I could do whatever I wanted within the limits of safety and carefulness, and she would still love me and be proud of me even if the other children there weren't. This was very important to me. When I knew that she supported me, it was easier to face the other kids at school.

Gabrielle's mother also helped her role-play various ways of responding when the other kids tried to exclude her or discourage her from doing what she wanted to do, and she says that that was very helpful to her when similar situations came up later. Gabrielle's mother seems to epitomize, in these scenes, the sort of response that Debold, Wilson, and Malave argue will make a real difference to a girl. Seen in this context, the strength Gabrielle exhibits at eleven, the way she vows to hold on to herself even as she heads into adolescence, is less mysterious. Her mother undoubtedly has a lot to do with it.

AT FOURTEEN, ANDI has spent most of her life as a home-schooler, with occasional forays into school. She spent kindergarten and first grade at home, went into school for second and third grade, left again for homeschooling until seventh grade (when she went to school for part of the year), and she is now auditing a couple of sophomore classes at the high school. Andi goes into school when she is curious about what goes on there or is looking to make new friends. She is not legally enrolled as a full-time student, so her attendance at the classes is not mandatory, and she doesn't receive grades (or, when she does, they don't go on a permanent record). "I'm basically just there to learn," she explains, "and there's a lot less pressure on you if you're just there to learn."

Andi is able to take the institution of school on her own terms, as the educational critic and homeschooling advocate John Holt put it. Being a homeschooler gives her the power to use school as she chooses to. If learning without grades removes the pressure for her, she can choose to audit her classes. She can decide which subjects to take in school and which not to take. Thus, even when she interacts with an institution that does *not* give young people much autonomy or decision-making power, Andi's status as a homeschooler allows her much more control over how she uses that institution than the other students have.

Like Gabrielle, Andi also has the freedom to distance herself from school's prevailing norms and assumptions. Andi says that her friends at school share her perspective and are similarly critical of the way school regulates and confines young people, so they are likely to support her, and her energy is not spent resisting *their* rules and norms as much as Gabrielle's was. She did have to challenge social norms when she refused to participate in the fight, as I described in chapter 4. Still, that

was during after-school hours. When she talks about the
school day, the rules and attitudes she describes herself questioning are those that come from the institution rather than
from her peer group. I ask Andi what bothers her about
school—why she doesn't just enroll full time, for example—
and she says, "Because I can't deal with the way they treat
people. They don't treat them like people, they treat them like
sheep. You know, they plot them: 'This is the way you're going
to be, don't try to be different.'" High school teachers give
students more freedom than teachers in the younger grades,
Andi explains, but "they do still treat you like subhumans, like
prehumans, you know, as soon as you graduate, then you can
be human."

I'm trying to imagine Andi putting up with high school's
rules and regulations, so I ask her if she ever challenges the
ones that bother her. She laughs and says she does indeed
challenge both the rules and the attitudes. "I got in trouble
for going to my locker," she begins.

> I had a pass for [going to] my locker. I went to the locker,
> grabbed what I needed out of my locker—it was some books to
> return to the library—and I stopped at the bathroom on the way
> back to the library. I got in trouble. And I fought! I was like, "I
> went to the bathroom without a pass, and you give me deten-
> tion? This is not right. This is why I was here, this is why I
> didn't have a pass." "Well, I've heard all that," [the teacher said].

Andi tried to argue, to get a hearing, but the teacher just
got angry at what he probably perceived as a typically sassy,
rebellious teenager who disobeys rules and challenges a
teacher's authority. Andi in fact wasn't actually disobeying a
rule, unless you assume that the pass that allowed her to be
out of class was strictly a locker pass and not a bathroom pass.
If this was the case then Andi was technically disobedient,
although the rule in question certainly seems petty when seen
in these terms. At any rate, it reveals the extent of the regi-
mentation of high school life. Really, Andi was objecting to
the indignity of having to justify her stop at the bathroom,

and perhaps it's because she doesn't take such indignities for granted that she was able to protest it.

Later Andi tells about a classroom discussion of school rules. "One of our teachers was reading us the rules and we were discussing them," she says, "and he was like, [students] can't be disrespectful. [The class had] a big blow-up of an argument, about, well, teachers are disrespectful to us, like we'll ask you a question and you won't answer it. That's disrespectful!"

Perhaps ironically, Andi is actually in favor of combining part-time school with homeschooling, and she recommends that other homeschoolers try school at some point. "Just to know the school system, to know why [school kids] act the way they do," she explains. When it comes to understanding both homeschooling and school, "You've got to know the difference, by experience," Andi believes. She advises that homeschoolers try school to find out "what you are missing or what you might not be missing. Go into somebody else's shoes and go: I like this, I don't like this, I can see why they might believe this but I still don't agree with it." Find out for yourself, Andi is saying. Investigate school and see what you think. Challenge its assumptions if you need to, either from the inside or out. "Homeschooling makes it so you can be free," Andi concludes. "A lot freer than everybody else." In context it's evident that the kind of freedom Andi is referring to is the freedom to question things, to explore various viewpoints and decide where you stand. She prefers to approach school as a homeschooler, with the distance and perspective that implies, but she would rather approach school in this way than never approach it at all, never experience it firsthand.

I've said that because Gabrielle and Andi spent so much less time in school compared to regularly enrolled students that they were able to keep from being fully absorbed by it. Fifteen-year-old Serena Gingold, however, enrolled in ninth grade full-time after homeschooling for her entire life. After she had been in school a few months, she had occasion to speak up, to act as a resister, and she described the experience in the newsletter her family publishes, the *Homeschoolers for Peace Pen-Pal Network:*

> I have never been sexually harassed myself, but a few weeks ago one of my friends was. We were sitting together on the bus ride and the two guys sitting behind us (both of whom I know) started making sexual remarks. One kept repeating in a sing-song voice that he wanted to have sex with my friend. She is very shy and kind and wouldn't stand up for herself. So I promptly told the two boys that they were sexually harassing her and that they had better stop. They replied by telling me to mind my own business and if my friend wanted them to stop she'd tell them so herself. They implied that she really liked it, but I knew she was very upset and embarrassed. I repeated what I had said earlier, adding that she wasn't the kind of person who talks back to anyone.
>
> Then the boy started verbally attacking me by yelling things like, "All that sexual harassment stuff is B.S.!" and "You'd better not try to sue me. Do that to the wrong person and you'll get yourself raped." Every high school boy on the bus was shaking his head in agreement. I asked him if he was threatening me, but he wouldn't respond. Pretty soon all the boys were yelling at me, and I was yelling back at them, defending myself and trying to explain to them how awful sexual harassment makes girls feel.
>
> What really surprised me was that NOT ONE high school girl said *anything.* There were no cries of "Sexual harassment should stop!" "I don't like it either!" or "There are laws against it!" I found that I had to do all the talking with no support. I don't think I made any of the boys want to stop sexually harassing girls, but I know that they'll never mess with me again, because they know I can hold my own.[63]

Serena is not bringing a homeschooling attitude, per se, into the school environment, but she is bringing a strength and an activism that I think is at least partially attributable to her homeschooling. Together, though in different ways, Gabrielle, Andi, and Serena suggest answers to the question of how possible it is for homeschoolers to maintain their resistance within the school environment.

It's not clear that any of them actually succeeded in making any changes in that environment, however. It would be nice to imagine that Gabrielle caused her teachers to reflect on sex-role stereotypes later on; perhaps at some point down the road, reading about girls in school, they remembered Gabrielle's comment and reconsidered their response. But this is very wishful thinking. Similarly, it would be nice to imagine that the other girls gained strength from Serena's example, and that may turn out to be true at some later point (especially if Serena keeps acting that way), but Serena's astonishment lay primarily in the fact that the other girls seemed either unable or unwilling to support her. She was very much the lone resister, the lone activist, in the scene on the school bus. With all three of the girls I have described here, what comes through most clearly is their ability to maintain themselves and their beliefs while in school, rather than their ability to change others' attitudes and behaviors.

Twelve-year-old Zoë Blowen-Ledoux was also the lone resister when she went into school for the first time. She didn't go in expecting to be a resister; she went in to see if she could do traditional schoolwork and to find a community of friends. "I dreamt of spending days in a row with friends, working on common projects and discussing meaningful ideas," she told *Growing Without Schooling*.[64] Yet when Zoë went to school she was surprised by what she found out about the other students and by what she found out about herself. She was successful academically, but "as it turned out," she says now, "I didn't like it or care. . . . For me, the grades were meaningless and everyone's intensity and anxiety about them were exhausting." She disliked the fact that only the academic stars were given awards at the end of the year.

When Zoë confronted the cliques—such a standard feature of middle school life for most girls—she was confused and disturbed. The emphasis on "wearing the right clothes, putting others down, collecting boys and 'friends' (allies in the social wars against each other) all took precedence over individuals' sense of right and wrong," Zoë recalls. She felt herself to be "in constant conflict with myself over my sense of appropriate behavior as opposed to what I could clearly see was acceptable and expected." She was upset when a girl in the class was "regularly ostracized and cruelly teased" and when the teachers did nothing to intervene. "It wasn't funny that I felt forced to be silent about how Samantha was treated," Zoë says now. She remembers that halfway through the year, she

> took a stand against this abuse. I tried to talk the girls out of it, but they just ignored me. When I shared my concern with the middle school director, her response was, "I don't want to make it worse by drawing attention to her. I'm hoping it will go away by itself." So much for community! Needless to say, the problem didn't go away. All the students knew they had permission to go on harassing her.

Naomi Wolf's analysis of girls' social organization, which I described in chapter 3, is right on target here. Zoë's dissent from the norms of the group was penalized, as Wolf suggests, and she got no reinforcement for "taking an unpopular view, challenging the status quo, or sticking to a conviction in the face of general condemnation." But it wasn't only the other girls who failed to support Zoë when she dared to speak up in defense of her own sense of right and wrong. The school authorities were no more supportive. In fact, in other ways—not just in regard to this one situation—the school authorities gave Zoë the message that it was important to blend in, to be like everyone else. "Another source of stress for me was a teacher who, on more than one occasion, humiliated me for being a vegetarian. He saw *me* as being unreasonable and overly difficult. He sure didn't see my differentness as special."

Because Zoë had been a homeschooler and had the option of becoming one again, she didn't have to see cliques and cliquish behavior as a natural or inevitable part of a teenager's life. When she returned to homeschooling the following year, she began publishing a newsletter for homeschoolers called *Self-Schooler's Network News.* She discovered that internships were another way to explore the wider world and find her community, and she became actively involved in local theater. Despite how difficult the school experience was for her, Zoë does not regret going because it taught her that she could stick with something difficult and because it showed her that the fantasy she'd had of school life was very different from the reality.

EVEN THOUGH HOMESCHOOLERS who go into school seem able only to maintain their own resistance, rather than to encourage it in others, the ability to maintain one's own resistance is no small thing. Abby, who has homeschooled since she was very young, is not convinced that she would be able to resist school's prevailing attitudes if she went to school with everyone else. When I ask her the standard interview question about what she has in common with friends who go to school, she mentions common interests. When I ask her how she differs from these friends, she says, "The major thing is I'm a lot freer." I ask in what ways.

> Timewise, emotionally-wise, and mentally-wise. In school, I think they have to worry a lot more about what kids think, because there's so many kids there, and they worry all the time about getting teased for being different and stuff. And I won't say that if I went to school, I wouldn't be like that, that I wouldn't worry about what kids thought. I mean, it'd be nice to say, no, I'd be the same person, but I'm not sure that's true. I might actually start worrying about it.

> *If you went to school right now, you mean?*

> Yeah, if I went to a high school. I am going to be going full-time starting in the summer, to college, but that's a very different environment. Everybody there sort of encourages you to be different, which is nice.

> *But you're guessing that if you went to high school right now, you might be just as vulnerable to—*

Well, no, I don't think I would be at *this* point, but I think that if I had gone, say, in ninth grade or something, then I might be. I really don't know, since fortunately for me I never did it [laughs].

Part of Abby seems to think it's mostly circumstance that frees her from the worries about what others will think. She's not so quick to say that she, herself, is strong enough to resist all the pressures that other kids succumb to, if she were to be in the same environment that they are in. On the other hand, when Abby thinks about it for a minute, she realizes that at sixteen and after so many years of being independent, she probably would be able to maintain that stance. I too would consider that a safe bet, given what Abby has told me about how she handled the party with the alcohol drinkers, for example. At the same time, her comment is a reminder that it's not so easy to say that homeschoolers can take what strengths they may have and run with them under all circumstances. Abby seems to be saying that she needed enough time to develop that strength fully. Her reflections pose a warning to homeschooling parents who think that homeschooling for just a couple of years can help a child become resilient enough to withstand the various pressures or challenges of schooling. Of course, for some kids under some circumstances, even a very short-term experience with homeschooling *can* serve as a break, a way of gaining perspective. What Abby is saying, however, is that people are indeed affected by their environment and by the attitudes of the people around them.

Abby was only speculating about how going into high school would affect her. Nineteen-year-old Jessica Spicer, in an interview in *Growing Without Schooling*, told about going into school for the first time at ninth grade.[65] Jessica enrolled because the school would not otherwise let her play on the high school gymnastics team, and she says that although she would have preferred only to be on the team, she enrolled as a full-time student and ended up making the honor roll and being in the popular social group. She says,

When I first started school, I was a teacher's pet. I was genuinely interested, I wanted to learn, and it was a big challenge. That's how it was at home—math was an exciting adventure. That attitude lasted for a while in school until I noticed that no one else was acting that way. The teachers sort of singled me out because they detected that I had energy and was interested. After a while I stopped showing my interest; I slipped into the background. Being interested isn't encouraged by the students. It wasn't that anyone ever *said*, "Don't be so interested," but I felt that. I felt that it was looked down on.

I thought that I could go in and just be who I am, love learning, wear my hair any way I wanted, and that I would have the strength to be myself no matter what. But I just couldn't do it. I feel like I come from a pretty strong family—we're all individuals, have high self-esteem. But in school there were just so many people all acting the same that it was oppressive. I also think I felt like I needed to assimilate, because there were so many different things already about me.

When people in the homeschooling community are asked what happens if homeschoolers go to school, they usually say that they do well, which means that they adjust and succeed on school's terms. Onlookers would surely have said this of Jessica. But she didn't succeed on her *own* terms, and in fact she ended up violating her own principles and becoming someone she wasn't proud of. Instead of being able to ignore the attitudes she didn't like or share, instead of being able to resist changing into someone she didn't want to be, Jessica found it difficult not to let the dominant culture of school overwhelm her.

At the end of the year, Jessica decided not to return to school. "A big reason was the effect school had on the relationship between my family and me," she explains.

When I was in school, I felt my family was weird or different, and then once I was out, they became my friends again, the people I enjoyed being with. I also noticed I was becoming—well, shallow, or I wasn't really thinking anymore. My thinking was devoted to

*169*

clothing choices or writing papers for the grade, not because I loved doing it. When I first went in, I thought I wasn't going to worry about my grades at all, but throughout the course of the year they became very important to me.

Jessica's story is an important reminder that even though some people within the homeschooling community may want to say that homeschoolers can bring their resistance into school, this isn't always easy or even possible. Although Jessica does say in her interview that she is glad she tried school because it gave her perspective and helped her understand what the experience was all about (much as Andi advocated), her story is more critical of that experience than many adult advocates of homeschooling would dare to be. Diplomacy might lead us to temper our stories, but there's no honest way to temper what Gabrielle shows us about sex-role stereotypes, what Serena shows us about sexual harassment, what Jessica shows us about attitudes toward learning.

I SAID THAT the girls who *were* able to bring their resistance into school were not particularly able to make changes within the school; at best, they were able to resist being changed themselves. There may be homeschoolers who do manage to make changes or affect others' views when they go into school either for specific activities or as full-time students, and this would be interesting to study. Meanwhile, I do know that some homeschoolers have been able to influence school policy from the vantage point of being a homeschooler; that is to say, after having left the system they are able to articulate their dissatisfaction with it and, sometimes, to get someone to pay attention. Sarah Clough's example is a striking one. Sarah left school at the beginning of tenth grade, and after she had been out for a few months she wrote a letter to the school superintendent asking why no one had taken any notice of her leaving or her reasons for doing so. Many homeschoolers consider it a good sign if local school officials don't pay much attention to them, because they would rather be left to homeschool without the district's monitoring or requirements. But Sarah felt that when she was a student she had tried many times to let the principal and other officials know about the problems she was facing, and she was frustrated that they didn't seem to take her seriously. Even after she had left school, she still wanted the people there to understand what had been going on and why she had left.

Sarah told *Growing Without Schooling* [66] that she had been the target of both physical and verbal attacks by other students, as had many others around her, and she found the school environment increasingly uncomfortable and even hostile. After repeated attempts to get some kind of help from school officials, Sarah said, "'Forget it, no one's going to do anything about this and I can't learn anymore.' When I sat in class I would be terrified that someone was waiting outside the door to say something to me or bully me, and I couldn't concentrate that way." She had heard about homeschooling and so decided to try it.

After Sarah wrote her letter to the school superintendent, he asked to meet with her, and Sarah reports that they had an interesting meeting in which she felt listened to and respected. Among other ideas, the superintendent suggested creating a group of students and teachers who would help mediate disputes or deal with the kind of bullying Sarah had faced. He invited Sarah to be part of that group, which she said she would certainly consider, and to return to school, which she said no longer interested her. Although when Sarah left school she had no particular thought about what homeschooling itself could give her, "Everything I do counts now, not just what I do for the grade or for the test," she explains, referring to the way that homeschooling allows her to choose what to learn and doesn't enforce rigid distinctions between school work and outside interests. "It makes you feel more important that way," Sarah continues, "More a part of the world and not just of school." She has no immediate plans to return to school, but she says she is glad she has gotten involved in trying to make changes there, both because it may help the students she left behind and because it helps her come to terms with her feelings about the past.

SOME HOMESCHOOLERS WHO don't choose to or aren't able to influence school officials as directly as Sarah did make a point of trying to communicate their perspective to the general public and to affect public attitudes. I've talked a lot about homeschoolers' having to defend themselves when others ask questions that are skeptical or even critical of homeschooling. Not all homeschoolers see this as burdensome (or perhaps it would be more accurate to say that not all homeschoolers see it this way all the time), and some place a high priority on trying to make themselves understood and on helping others understand what alternatives are available to them. Homeschooling parents have for years written articles, given talks, and spoken with newspaper, radio, and television reporters, and homeschooling children and teenagers increasingly join in these efforts as well.

Nell, at sixteen, found that staying true to her own beliefs involved resisting school's—and in a sense the culture's—standards and expectations. In choosing not to take the Scholastic Aptitude Test (SAT) in spite of wanting to go to college, Nell was bringing her resistance into school in a less direct way than the others I've described so far. She wasn't actually enrolled in school when she went on college interviews and explained her decision not to take the SAT, but she was certainly engaging with the institution of school and explaining her unusual choice.

"I guess it all started when I took the eighth-grade test, the way we're state-mandated to do," Nell begins, referring to the standardized test that homeschoolers in her state are required to take periodically. "I did very well on it, which I thought at the time was a lot of hoopla [about] nothing, because I knew from the beginning how little how I did on the test reflected what I knew." Two years later, when her mother reminded her that it would soon be time to register for the Preliminary Scholastic Aptitude Test (PSAT), Nell hesitated and let the date go by. The following year, when most people her age who were college-bound were taking the SAT, Nell decided that she "absolutely did not want to take" that test. She refused partly because she objected to standardized testing ("I *hate* the idea of being measured by a score") and partly because she wasn't thoroughly convinced that the SAT stood between her and what she wanted to do, and she didn't want to take it unless that correlation became clear to her. Though, as Nell says, homeschoolers in her state are required to take standardized tests periodically, they take them less often than students in school do, and Nell's homeschooling does not place the emphasis that school places on tests in general. Nell hates the idea of being measured by a score because in her homeschooling, she does not measure herself in standardized terms, but rather in terms of her own growth, development, and progress in various areas over time.

"It came closer to being SAT time," Nell remembers, "and Mom was saying, if you want to do this, you should start studying, and all I could think of was, why? I mean, what do I want that these will help me get?"

High school students probably ask themselves why they are taking the SAT, but more often than not they ask it jokingly or ironically, as when they ask why they are doing many of the tasks they consider meaningless but obligatory. They don't ask the question with the assumption that they can truly do anything about the answer. But for Nell the question was real and was engendered by the power she already knew she possessed to make important choices about her life.

Nell could have answered the question by saying, "Because I want to go to a four-year college." Other homeschoolers have given that answer and gone on to take the SAT with that goal clearly in mind. Nell knew that not all colleges require the SAT, however, and furthermore she wasn't sure that she wanted to enroll in college full-time. At that point, she imagined herself taking one or two classes a semester while continuing with her job and with other activities that were important to her (she was only the age of a high school senior at this point, anyway). She said that if her goals radically changed and she decided that she did want to go to a college that required the SAT with no exceptions, she would consider taking it. She was not interested in sabotaging her own goals for the sake of a principle, but she wasn't interested in violating a principle for no clear reason, either.

Nell then began going on college interviews, and in some cases the interviewers didn't know that she was interested primarily in part-time enrollment.

> I told four admissions people that I hadn't taken the SATs and didn't anticipate taking them, and nobody went through the roof despite the fact that the college books all said "SAT or ACT scores required for admittance" or "99% of the student body submits SAT scores" or whatever. . . . One of the [admissions officers] did say, why have you chosen to do that, or why haven't you taken the test, and I said, you know, if it becomes really important to me, and this is the only way that I can accomplish my dream or my wish, then I'm going to reevaluate. [But in the meantime], I know that I've had a very nontraditional education, and I've found that—it's been my experience that—if you give someone a test score, they're more likely to look at it and see the test score and not the person. And I wanted very much not to be a number, but to be a person, and that was one of the reasons I was interviewing in person, and why I had not submitted an SAT score. I tried to be very tactful about it.

Nell ended up taking one class at a selective liberal arts college that doesn't ordinarily admit part-time students, and then, the following semester, two classes at a larger university. So far, she is able to live the kind of life she wants to live without having to compromise and take the SAT, and from everything she's said about herself, this kind of quiet but definite resistance to societal pressures and expectations is characteristic of her approach. She says, "Most people who know me don't think of me as a rebellious person," and yet she also knows that most people don't understand her decision not to take the test that so many other college-bound students take. As with her decision to stop dancing ballet in public, Nell's decision not to take the SAT was not a response to "most people" but rather something she undertook for herself.

# Conclusion

"*I* like how I've learned, I like who I am, I like what I know," says Andi. "I'm not going to let what people think I ought to be influence what I'm going to be," says Gabrielle. "I know what I think and feel and I have my beliefs and don't let myself get pushed around," says Claudia. Throughout this book the homeschooled girls I've interviewed have echoed these statements. They have talked about trusting themselves, pursuing their own goals, maintaining friendships even when their friends differ from them or disagree with them. In the context of the general discussion about adolescent girls, these voices are discordant, but it is a useful kind of discord, a discord that says there is hope, resistance is possible, and not all girls are suffering or have to suffer.

To take the hope these girls are offering and truly make something out of it, however, we have to look at how it has arisen and what has made it possible. In the introduction to her book *SchoolGirls: Young Women, Self-Esteem, and the Confidence Gap*, journalist Peggy Orenstein writes,

> Although ideas about the importance of self-esteem have been knocking around academic literature since the late nineteenth century, the phrase has become the buzzword of the 1990s. . . . I started out a critic of the self-esteem evangelists. I was suspicious of any movement that stressed personal transformation over structural change, especially for women. Self-esteem sounded to me like another way to blame the victim, warm fuzzy style. We do girls a disservice, I reasoned, if we encourage them to feel good about themselves rather than targeting the overarching institutions, policies, and cultural attitudes that make them (understandably) feel worthless.
>
> . . . But spending time in the world of girls (and reflecting on the world of women) convinced me that the internal need not, and indeed should not, be ignored.[67]

I agree that the internal feelings and perceptions of girls and women should not be ignored, but I do not see how they can be considered in a productive way if the external structures are not also examined. I once received a mailing about recordings that were going to be broadcast over a school's public address system periodically throughout the day. They would say phrases like, "I am capable," "My feelings are important," and so forth, with the goal of increasing the students' self-esteem. Meanwhile, these students were at the same time receiving very different messages from the school system itself. If this school was in any way typical, it is likely that the students were not allowed to make many significant choices (about what to learn or about when to go to the bathroom), did not feel that their preferences were taken into account, did not feel respected or listened to or powerful or important.

Students will not feel capable and important simply because they continually hear, and perhaps learn to repeat, statements to that effect. The structure and assumptions of schooling speak more loudly and persuasively than anything that may be broadcast over its PA systems (or even said by its teachers). If, in thinking about these issues, we discover that there is a contradiction between what we say to young people and what the school system itself communicates, that contradiction is what needs our attention.

In fact, Peggy Orenstein's account of a year spent in two middle schools—one suburban, wealthy, and mostly white, and the other urban, poor, and mostly African American and Latino—does look closely at what school communicates to girls and how difficult it is for girls in *both* school environments to be nourished, supported, and heard. The AAUW research (which was the basis for Orenstein's work) looks at the effects of school's practices and methods, and the research from the Harvard project looks at school's effects to some extent, although less directly. But none of this is the same as looking at what it means that girls (or any young people) go to school at all. None of this research looks at the structure and assumptions of schooling as a whole.

If one has thought seriously about the structure and assumptions of compulsory schooling, it is hard to read the psychological literature that asks, "How can we get girls to identify with their own goals?" or even "How can we help girls to discover their own real interests?" without thinking about the fact that school is in direct opposition to these concerns. People may say or believe that school is about helping young people discover and pursue their own goals, but in fact school tells students what to learn and when and how, and it penalizes them if they do not comply with these demands. Going to school is about following someone else's plan, someone else's timetable, someone else's methods. People in school do not say to the students, "What can we do for you? How would you like to make use of this institution?" On the contrary, going to school is about *getting* an education—having something given or done *to* you.

The homeschooled girls I have described are outside this framework. They are not waiting to get something; rather, they are getting it or, more aptly, making it for themselves. When they say, "Everything I do counts now," or, "I feel so much freer," or, "I mainly teach myself," these are not just feelings they happen to have. These statements actually correspond with the external structure of these girls' lives. Everything they do does count; it's not as if they will only get credit for some books or activities or learning and not for others. The girls in this book who have left school and are now homeschooling *are* much freer, in that they have greater liberty to choose what to learn and to learn it in ways that work for them. The girls who say, "I mainly teach myself," are saying something true; the structure of their homeschooling does allow them to be primarily their own teachers. Thus, the relationship between the external facts and these internal feelings is reciprocal and not coincidental.

The relationship between the external facts of the lives of girls in school and *their* internal feelings makes sense as well. Too often, adolescents learn exactly what their environment teaches them and are then blamed for having learned it too

well. Adults often criticize adolescents for having a herd mentality, for example, for ostracizing those who are different and
not valuing individual variety. Looking for the source of these
attitudes, adults tend to look first at the adolescent peer culture and then only at how that culture exists in school. But as
I suggested when I discussed the function of cliques, the adolescent peer culture may be an adaptive response rather than
a cause. Are schools traditionally characterized by a herd
mentality? Do they deal with young people in groups or as
individuals? Can a school—not necessarily specific teachers,
but the school system in general—handle different styles or
rates of learning? What happens when one child can read
when the others in the classroom can't, or vice versa? Are
many ways of getting an answer welcomed in most class-
rooms, or are students told that they must all work in the
same way?

Similarly, it is so difficult for most people to understand
what homeschoolers mean when they say they teach themselves, are able to learn in ways that work for them, and value
"the freedom to choose [their] own goals and work toward
them in [their] own way" because these attitudes are not what
education is usually all about. Is school set up to allow students
to choose their own goals or to work toward the same goal in
varying ways? What about choosing their learning materials or
wanting to learn from people other than the school's teachers?
Or dropping a subject that is no longer of interest?

Some people, reading about the qualities and attributes of
the homeschooled adolescent girls I interviewed, might not
consider those qualities particularly significant. For people
who believe (as many people do) that education is about pro-
ceeding without mishap down a predetermined path, the idea
of young people being able to make choices and to discover
what they truly love is not important. In fact, many consider
it dangerous.

Other people, however, may find the qualities that many of
the girls in this book possess desirable and worth cultivating.
Many psychologists, educators, and parents worry nowadays

about the findings of the research to which I have been referring throughout this book. They worry when girls do not seem able to develop their strengths, value their own points of view, or make choices that matter to them. It is to these people that I feel I am especially speaking when I say that we need to acknowledge the contradiction between what we say we want and what the school system actually communicates. If we want young people to tolerate difference and disagreement, the school system itself must actually tolerate it as well, even if that means acknowledging that students do not learn in the same way or that they may disagree with the teachers or with each other. If we want girls to be able to look to their own authority and not always to an external authority, we have to structure school in such a way that it is not always the external authority that holds the answers or determines when something is completed or learned or done well enough. If we want girls to identify with the goals they are pursuing, we have to give them the opportunity to choose goals with which they *do* identify and then to pursue those goals with our help. And again, if there is at present a great gap between what we want school to communicate and what school does in fact communicate, that is where the work needs to be done. If doing that work only reveals that many adults do not share these goals—do not think that the interests, needs, and feelings of young people are of primary importance—well, at least then we can be having that discussion and understanding that *that* disagreement is where the real problem lies.

MEREDITH, APPLYING TO college a year after I interviewed her, wrote in one of her application essays that

> My outlook on life has been affected in many, many ways by homeschooling.... I have grown up in an atmosphere of tolerance for individuality. Kids in school can have a hard time discovering who they are, in part because they have only other kids to compare themselves to. If all the other kids are the same (externally), it can be scary to be seen as different in any way.

I have had the chance to become a strong individual and to know who I am, if not who I will be. In the past three years I have been living in what I would call "real life," interacting with people in many different situations and coming to a thorough understanding of myself and why I do what I do.

Homeschooling can give young people the chance to ask the question, "Who am I? What do I really want?" It is through the process of asking and then gradually *answering* that question that the girls I've interviewed have developed the strengths and the resistance abilities that give them such an unusually strong sense of self. They can say, "I like who I am," not just because they have learned to repeat such a statement but because they have had a chance to think about who they would like to be and to work at becoming that person. This is the chance I would like to see all young people have.

# Notes

1. See, for example, Carol Gilligan, Nona Lyons, and Trudy Hammer, eds., *Making Connections: The Relational Worlds of Adolescent Girls at Emma Willard School*, (Cambridge: Harvard University Press, 1990); Carol Gilligan, Annie Rogers, and Deborah Tolman, eds., *Women, Girls, and Psychotherapy: Reframing Resistance* (New York: The Haworth Press, 1991); and Lyn Mikel Brown and Carol Gilligan, *Meeting at the Crossroads: Women's Psychology and Girls' Development*, (Cambridge: Harvard University Press, 1992).

2. American Association of University Women, *Shortchanging Girls, Shortchanging America: A Call to Action*, (Washington, DC: AAUW, 1991), p. 11, and American Association of University Women, *How Schools Shortchange Girls*, (Washington, DC: AAUW, 1992), p. 12.

3. Myra and David Sadker, *Failing at Fairness: How America's Schools Cheat Girls*, (New York: Macmillan, 1994).

4. Elizabeth Debold, Marie Wilson, and Idelisse Malave, *The Mother Daughter Revolution: From Betrayal to Power* (Reading, MA: Addison-Wesley, 1993), p. xiv.

5. Debold, Wilson, and Malave, p. 7.

6. For a fuller description of this work, see Susannah Sheffer, *Writing Because We Love To: Homeschoolers at Work* (Portsmouth, NH: Heinemann, 1992).

7. Jessica Gray, "The Journey from School to Homeschooling," *Growing Without Schooling #93*, 16, no. 2, (June 1993): 10–11.

8. Vivien Zapf, "What Socialization Means," *Growing Without Schooling #88*, 15, no. 3 (August 1992): 23.

9. For a particularly in-depth example, see Patrick Meehan in *Real Lives: Eleven Teenagers Who Don't Go to School*, ed. Grace Llewellyn. (Eugene, OR: Lowry House, 1993).

10. American Association of University Women, *How Schools Shortchange Girls*, p. 32.

11. Debold, Wilson, and Malave, p. xvi.

12. Carol Gilligan, prologue to *Making Connections: The Relational Worlds of Adolescent Girls at Emma Willard School*, eds. Gilligan, Lyons, and Hammer. (Cambridge: Harvard University Press, 1990).

13. American Association of University Women, *Short-changing Girls, Shortchanging America*, p. 4.

14. Lori Stern, "Disavowing the Self in Female Adolescence," in *Women, Girls, and Psychotherapy: Reframing Resistance*, eds. Gilligan, Rogers, and Tolman (New York: The Haworth Press, 1991), pp. 105–115.

15. Tabitha Mountjoy, "Studies on Her Own," *Growing Without Schooling #81*, 14, no. 3. (June 1991): 14.

16. Lura Lee Roberts, "In the World of Work," *Growing Without Schooling #81*, 14, no. 3 (June 1991): 5.

17. Emily Bergson-Shilcock, "Volunteer Experiences," *Growing Without Schooling, #95*, 16, no. 4 (October 1993): 8–9.

18. Olivia Baseman, "What Kind of Help Is Helpful," *Growing Without Schooling #80*, 14, no. 2 (April 1991): 22.

19. Amber Heintzberger, "Working Toward a Goal," *Growing Without Schooling #84*, 14, no. 6 (December 1991): 14.

20. Quoted in Debold, Wilson, and Malave, p. 54.

21. Brown and Gilligan, p. 5.

22. American Association of University Women, *How Schools Shortchange Girls*, pp. 12–13.

23. For particularly vivid descriptions of these different responses to adolescence by white, African American,

and Latina girls, see Peggy Orenstein, *SchoolGirls: Young Women, Self-Esteem, and the Confidence Gap* (New York: Doubleday, 1994).

24. Debold, Wilson, and Malave, p. 14.

25. American Association of University Women, *How Schools Shortchange Girls*, pp. 12–13.

26. Jane O'Reilly, "The Lost Girls," *Mirabella* (April 1994): 117–20

27. For a further discussion of African American home-schoolers, see Ayanna Williams in *Real Lives: Eleven Teenagers Who Don't Go to School* (Eugene, OR: Lowry House, 1993) and Donna Nichols-White and Kristin Cleage Williams, "African-American Homeschoolers," *Growing Without Schooling #88*, 15, no. 3 (August 1992). There are now two newsletters specifically by and for homeschoolers of color: *Umoja\*Unidad\*Unity* and *The Drinking Gourd*.

28. In both Carol Gilligan, "Joining the Resistance: Psychology, Politics, Girls, and Women," *Michigan Quarterly Review*, 29, no. 4 (1991): 501–36, and Brown and Gilligan, p. 223.

29. See, for example, Katherine McAlpine, "Being a Single Parent," *Growing Without Schooling #58*, 10, no. 4 (August 1, 1987): 5–6; Victoria Moran, "How a Single Parent Homeschools," *Growing Without Schooling #90*, 15, no. 5 (December 1, 1992): 8–9, and "Single-Parent Homeschoolers," *Growing Without Schooling #84*, 14, no. 6 (December 1, 1991): 5–6.

30. See, for example, "Two-Career Families," *Growing Without Schooling #77*, 13, no. 5 (October 1, 1990): 7–8; "Work and Financial Arrangements," *Growing Without Schooling #97*, 16, no. 6 (February 1, 1994): 10–13; "Children in the Workplace," *Growing Without Schooling #64*, 11, no. 4, (August 1, 1988): 22–23.

31. Debold, Wilson, and Malave, pp. 184–85

32. Debold, Wilson, and Malave, p. 134.

33. Unpublished letter.

34. Quoted in John Holt, *Teach Your Own* (New York: Delacorte, 1981), p. 133.

35. Maggi Elliott, "Feminist Homeschoolers," *Growing Without Schooling #75*, 13, no. 3 (June 1990): 6.

36. Sandee Resnick, "Feminist Homeschoolers," *Growing Without Schooling #75*, 13, no. 3 (June 1990): 6.

37. Unpublished letter.

38. Unpublished letter.

39. Unpublished letter.

40. Muriel Palko, "Feminist Homeschoolers," *Growing Without Schooling #75*, 13, no. 3 (June 1990): 6.

41. Unpublished letter.

42. Unpublished letter.

43. Press release from New Moon Publishing, February 1993.

44. Personal conversation with Nancy Gruver. For a fuller description of the effect that Gruver's and Kelly's experience as homeschooling parents had on the creation of *New Moon*, see Joe Kelly, "How Unschooling Led to *New Moon* Magazine," *Growing Without Schooling #100*, 17, no. 3 (July/August 1994): 28–29.

45. Debold, Wilson, and Malave, pp. 17–18

46. Beverly Jean Smith, "Raising a Resister," in *Women, Girls, and Psychotherapy: Reframing Resistance*, eds. Gilligan, Rogers, and Tolman (New York: The Haworth Press, 1991), pp. 137–48.

47. Terri Apter's book is *Altered Loves: Mothers and Daughters During Adolescence* (New York: Ballantine, 1990).

48. See, for example, Earl Stevens and David Swank, "Fathers at Home," *Growing Without Schooling #86*, 15, no. 2 (April 1, 1992): 9–10.

49. Anita Giesy, "Joining in School's Social Life," *Growing Without Schooling #77*, 13, no. 5 (October 1990): 19.

50. Debold, Wilson, and Malave, p. 40.

51. Brown and Gilligan, p. 50.

52. Ibid., p. 3.

53. Ibid., p. 58.

54. Naomi Wolf, *Fire with Fire* (New York: Random House, 1993), pp. 109–10.

55. Ibid, pp. 278–79.

56. Olivia Baseman, "Imagining the Future," *Growing Without Schooling #87*, 15, no. 3 (June 1992): p. 19.

57. Lyn Mikel Brown, "Telling a Girl's Life: Self-Authorization as a Form of Resistance," in *Women, Girls, and Psychotherapy: Reframing Resistance*, eds. Gilligan, Rogers, and Tolman (New York: The Haworth Press, 1991): p. 83.

58. Ibid., p. 80.

59. Debold, Wilson, and Malave, p. 43.

60. Ibid., p. 13.

61. Ibid., p. 43–44.

62. Ibid., p. 49.

63. Serena Gingold, "Stand Up Against Sexual Harassment," *Homeschoolers for Peace Pen-Pal Network*, January 1994.

64. Zoë Blowen-Ledoux, "Trying School," *Growing Without Schooling #99*, 17, no. 2 (May/June 1994): 29.

65. Jessica Spicer, "Trying School—And Leaving Again," *Growing Without Schooling #95*, 16, no. 4 (October 1993): 18–19.

66. Sarah Clough, "Letter to a Superintendent," *Growing Without Schooling #98*, 17, no. 1 (March/April 1994): 33–34.

67. Orenstein, p. xviii.

# References

American Association of University Women. 1991. *Shortchanging Girls, Shortchanging America: A Call to Action*. Washington, DC: AAUW.

————. 1992. *How Schools Shortchange Girls*. Washington, DC: AAUW.

Apter, Terri. 1990. *Altered Loves: Mothers and Daughters During Adolescence*. New York: Ballantine.

Baseman, Olivia. 1991. "What Kind of Help Is Helpful." *Growing Without Schooling #80* 14, no. 2 (April).

————. 1992. "Imagining the Future." *Growing Without Schooling #87*, 15, no. 3 (June).

Bergson-Shilcock, Emily. 1993. "Volunteer Experiences." *Growing Without Schooling #95*, 16, no. 4 (October).

Blowen-Ledoux, Zoë. 1994. "Trying School." *Growing Without Schooling #99*, 17, no. 2 (May/June).

Brown, Lyn Mikel. 1991. "Telling a Girl's Life: Self-Authorization as a Form of Resistance." In *Women, Girls, and Psychotherapy: Reframing Resistance*, edited by Carol Gilligan, Annie Rogers, and Deborah Tolman. New York: The Haworth Press.

Brown, Lyn Mikel and Carol Gilligan. 1992. *Meeting at the Crossroads: Women's Psychology and Girls' Development*. Cambridge: Harvard University Press.

Chideya, Garai. 1992. "Revolution, Girl Style." *Newsweek*, 120, no. 21 (November 23), p. 84.

Clough, Sarah. 1994. "Letter to a Superintendent." *Growing Without Schooling #98*, 17, no. 1 (March/April).

Debold, Elizabeth, Marie Wilson, and Idelisse Malave. 1993. *The Mother Daughter Revolution: From Betrayal to Power*. Reading, MA: Addison-Wesley.

Elliott, Maggi. 1990. "Feminist Homeschoolers." *Growing Without Schooling #75*, 13, no. 3 (June).

Giesy, Anita. 1990. "Joining in School's Social Life." *Growing Without Schooling #77*, 13, no. 5 (October).

Gilligan, Carol. 1991. "Joining the Resistance: Psychology, Politics, Girls, and Women." *Michigan Quarterly Review* 29, no. 4.

Gilligan, Carol, Annie Rogers, and Deborah Tolman, eds. 1991. *Women, Girls, and Psychotherapy: Reframing Resistance.* New York: The Haworth Press.

Gilligan, Carol, Nona Lyons, and Trudy Hammer, eds. 1990. *Making Connections: The Relational Worlds of Girls at Emma Willard School.* Cambridge: Harvard University Press.

Gingold, Serena. 1994. "Stand Up Against Sexual Harassment." *Homeschoolers for Peace Pen-Pal Network* (January).

Gray, Jessica. 1993. "The Journey from School to Homeschooling." *Growing Without Schooling #93*, 16, no. 2 (June).

Hancock, Emily. 1989. *The Girl Within.* New York: Ballantine.

Heintzberger, Amber. 1991. "Working Toward a Goal." *Growing Without Schooling #84*, 14, no. 6 (December).

Holt, John. 1981. *Teach Your Own.* New York: Delacorte.

Kelly, Joe. 1993. "Listening to Girls with Annie Rogers," *New Moon Parenting*, no. 1 (June/July).

Llewellyn, Grace, ed. 1993. *Real Lives: Eleven Teenagers Who Don't Go to School.* Eugene, OR: Lowry House.

Mountjoy, Tabitha. 1991. "Studies on Her Own." *Growing Without Schooling #81*, 14, no. 3 (June).

O'Reilly, Jane. 1994. "The Lost Girls." *Mirabella.* April.

Orenstein, Peggy. 1994. *SchoolGirls: Young Women, Self-Esteem, and the Confidence Gap.* New York: Doubleday.

Palko, Muriel. 1990. "Feminist Homeschoolers." *Growing Without Schooling #75*, 13, no. 3 (June).

Resnick, Sandee. 1990. "Feminist Homeschoolers." *Growing Without Schooling #75*, 13, no. 3 (June).

Roberts, Lura Lee. 1991. "In the World of Work." *Growing Without Schooling #81*, 14, no. 3 (June).

Sadker, Myra and David Sadker. 1994. *Failing at Fairness: How America's Schools Cheat Girls.* New York: Macmillan.

Sheffer, Susannah. 1992. *Writing Because We Love To: Homeschoolers at Work.* Portsmouth, NH: Heinemann.

Smith, Beverly Jean. 1991. "Raising a Resister." In *Women, Girls, and Psychotherapy: Reframing Resistance*, edited by Carol Gilligan, Annie Rogers, and Deborah Tolman. New York: The Haworth Press.

Spicer, Jessica. 1993. "Trying School—And Leaving Again." *Growing Without Schooling #95*, 16, no. 4 (October).

Stern, Lori. 1991. "Disavowing the Self in Female Adolescence." In *Women, Girls, and Psychotherapy: Reframing Resistance*, edited by Carol Gilligan, Annie Rogers, and Deborah Tolman. New York: The Haworth Press.

Wolf, Naomi. 1993. *Fire with Fire*. New York: Random House.

Zapf, Vivien. 1992. "What Socialization Means." *Growing Without Schooling #88*, 15, no. 3 (August).